Lecture Notes in Economics and Mathematical Systems

Managing Editors: M. Beckmann and H. P. Künzi

Econometrics

178

M. N. Bhattacharyya

Comparison of Box-Jenkins and Bonn Monetary Model Prediction Performance

Springer-Verlag
Berlin Heidelberg New York 1980

Editorial Board

H. Albach A. V. Balakrishnan M. Beckmann (Managing Editor)
P. Dhrymes J. Green W. Hildenbrand W. Krelle
H. P. Künzi (Managing Editor) K. Ritter R. Sato H. Schelbert
P. Schönfeld

Managing Editors

Prof. Dr. M. Beckmann
Brown University
Providence, RI 02912/USA

Prof. Dr. H. P. Künzi
Universität Zürich
CH-8090 Zürich/Schweiz

Author

M. N. Bhattacharyya
Department of Economics, University of Queensland
St. Lucia, Brisbane 4067/Australia

ISBN 3-540-10011-3 Springer-Verlag Berlin Heidelberg New York
ISBN 0-387-10011-3 Springer-Verlag New York Heidelberg Berlin

This work is subject to copyright. All rights are reserved, whether the whole or part of the material is concerned, specifically those of translation, reprinting, re-use of illustrations, broadcasting, reproduction by photocopying machine or similar means, and storage in data banks. Under § 54 of the German Copyright Law where copies are made for other than private use, a fee is payable to the publisher, the amount of the fee to be determined by agreement with the publisher.

© by Springer-Verlag Berlin Heidelberg 1980
Printed in Germany

Printing and binding: Beltz Offsetdruck, Hemsbach/Bergstr.
2142/3140-543210

PREFACE

The purpose of the present study is to evaluate the predictive performance of an earlier version of the Bonn Monetary Model ("Ein Ökonometrisches Vierteljahresmodell des Geld- und Kreditsektors für die Bundesrepublik Deutschland", by Jörn Martiensen (1975), Meisenheim, Verlag Anton Hain) against the benchmark provided by the Box-Jenkins univariate autoregressive-integrated moving average, ARIMA, model. Similar studies aimed at evaluating the predictive performance of the econometric models of the North American economies had been reported earlier. But to the best of my knowledge, no such works, at least up to the time, early 1976 when I took up the present investigation, had been done with any of the European econometric models, except Prothero and Wallis (1976), discussed in the introduction to the present book.

The previous studies of this type generated plenty of unconstructive and sometimes unpleasant dialogues. Neither do I appreciate the over-reaction of the econometricians when an econometric model is evaluated nor do I appreciate when it is said that econometrics is withering. According to my opinion, econometric model building is a great experimentation and univariate time series models are not expected to be substitutes for econometric models. But as the economic data are invariably in the form of time series, how can the econometricians, and why should they, ignore the results of time series analysis simply on the ground that such an analysis is not based on any of the fond theories. In fact time series analysis should be an integral part of econometrics. It should provide important information for model building and an objective yardstick for model evaluation.

Unlike previous researchers, I extended my study to explore the causal relationships, causality defined by Granger (1969), between the selected monetary variables. I think such an exercise is an imperative extension to this type of investigation.

The discussion on an econometric model should contain the analysis in detail. With this point in view I have appended the sample time series, analysis leading to the development of time series models, two sets of post sample forecasts, and composite forecasts along with the actual realizations. In this respect I did not follow the remarks of a reviewer that such a volume of data are redundant.

I like to add that I carried out the project of prediction evaluation with a sincere hope that the results of my analysis would help in improving the efficacy of the model. I am happy to learn that my work was not considered as a negative piece of work done by a 'Guest Professor' having no permanent interest in the Bonn Institute. In fact, I have been informed that partly due to the results of my work and partly due to other considerations, the monetary model, under evaluation in this book, has been replaced with a more efficient model for the monetary and credit systems, which forms a part of the Bonn Model Version 10 (K. Conard and P. Kohnert, "Economic Activity, Interest Rates and the Exchange Rate in the Bonn Forecasting System No. 10, Second Revision, February 1980). This revised and extended Bonn Model is now a part of the "Project Link". In this respect I would like to thank Professor Dr Wilhelm Krelle for taking such a positive attitude that the evaluation of a model is a constructive piece of work meant to start a process of thinking and rethinking leading to an improved version of the same. However, it should be made clear at this stage that in the subsequent discussions presented in this book I shall invariably refer to the 1975 versions of the Bonn Econometric Model and Bonn Monetary Model wherever they are mentioned.

I would like to take this opportunity to acknowledge thankfully the facilities and encouragement that I received from Professor Dr Wilhelm Krelle, Director, and Professor Dr Peter Schönfeld, Professor of Econometrics, Institute for Econometrics and Operations Research, University of Bonn, West Germany. Thanks are also due to Dr Martiensen for helpful discussion and Messrs Peter Brandenburg and Deiter Elixmann for computational assistance. Mrs Nicholai of the Bonn Institute and Ms Margaret Cowan, Jenny Randall, Caroline Verhoeven and Mrs Christine Ives of the Department of Economics, University of Queensland, deserve my thanks for the careful and painstaking typing and retyping of the manuscript.

Finally, I believe econometric model evaluation against Box-Jenkins model will be a routine practice in future and a publication in detail will be of use to the students and researchers.

M.N. Bhattacharyya
Department of Economics,
University of Queensland,
Brisbane, Australia.

November 1979.

CONTENTS

1.	Introduction	1
2.	Bonn econometric model of German economy	9
3.	ARIMA models for fifteen endogenous variables of the BNM model	11
4.	Analysis of sample period lead 1 forecast errors	15
5.	Bates-Granger composite forecast and its application in evaluating econometric model	20
6.	Analysis of post-sample lead 1 forecast errors	25
7.	Causal relationships between selected economic variables	30
7.1	Granger's definition of causality and its characterization	30
7.2	Detection of causality: Pierce's broad tests	36
7.2.1	Testing the independence of two series x and y: $\rho(uv;k) = 0$ for all k	37
7.2.2	Assessment of different types of causality	39
7.2.3	Confirmation of unidirectional causality	41
7.3	Causal relationships between the selected monetary variables of the BNM model	43
7.4	Progressive χ^2 tests for detecting causality	47
7.5	Causal relationships between short-term interest rate, 90-day money rate Frankfurt, and other selected variables	51
Bibliography		55
Appendix		63
Glossary of abbreviations used in BNM model		143
Index		145

1. INTRODUCTION

An econometric model of an economy consists of a large number of structural equations and identities specified on the basis of the model builder's theoretical knowledge and experience of the economy concerned. Each structural equation represents one aspect of the structure of the economic system and each identity represents either a definition or an equilibrium condition or an accounting equality. The set of all structural equations of a model is called the structural form. The structural form can be manipulated to reduced form where each endogenous variable can be expressed as a function of the lagged endogenous and exogenous variables and the stochastic disturbance terms of the original structural equations.

Since the equations of an econometric model are based on economic theories, they are expected to simulate jointly the behaviour of the economy as a whole. As such they are recommended to be used for economic decision and control. But before making use of them, it is desirable to evaluate objectively the level of their effectiveness for the specified purpose.

One of the methods of evaluation may be to calculate forecasts for the sample (fit period) and post-sample (outside the fit period) period with known realizations and examine the quality of the forecasts (Theil (1961)). Following the above procedure, Stekler (1968) attempted to evaluate the predictive performance of six quarterly models of the U.S. economy. He judged the accuracy of the forecasts by calculating Theil's inequality coefficient, called U coefficient. But as Stekler himself has pointed out, Theil's coefficient is not based on any statistical theory and as such does not provide a rigorous significance test. It is, therefore, not possible to judge whether the difference between two U coefficients is statistically significant. Stekler made a more or less subjective decision by comparing the calculated value of U coefficient of a model with a similar coefficient generated from naive or no-change forecasts.

Accuracy of forecasts is a subjective quality. What is an accurate forecast for one purpose may not be accurate enough for another purpose; similarly what is an accurate forecast to one person may not look accurate enough to another person. Therefore, a better procedure in this case may be to compare the forecasting efficiency of an econometric model with that of an alternative competing model and draw a conclusion on the basis of relative efficiency. To make this comparison valid it is desirable to select a legitimate contender. For example the competing model should be a stochastic model because the econometric models are stochastic models; secondly, the information set exploited by the competing model should be covered by the information set exploited by the econometric model which is to be evaluated.

The Box-Jenkins univariate autoregressive-integrated-moving average, ARIMA, models have recently emerged as valid contenders of the econometric models since they satisfy all the required qualifications specified above. Firstly, the ARIMA models are stochastic models; secondly, an ARIMA model of an endogenous variable exploits only the past history of the variable concerned while the corresponding econometric model is based simultaneously on the past history of the

variable itself and the past histories of the endogenous
and exogenous relatives; and in this sense the basic information set of the econometric model includes the basic information set of the ARIMA model. The ARIMA has other attractions also. It is specified empirically and has acquired a
reputation for producing short and medium range quality
forecasts. Since an ARIMA model is not based on any economic
or physical theory, it was initially dubbed as a naive model.
But recent researchers (Zellner & Palm (1974) and Prothero
& Wallis (1976)) have shown that through the notion of the
final equation, an ARIMA is related to the econometric
structural equation. Zellner and Palm at the end of a
commendable investigation remarked that 'so-called 'naive'
ARIMA time series models are not all that naive after all'.
However, naive or no naive, ARIMA provides an objective
benchmark against which the predictive performance of an
econometric model may be assessed.

Following the idea of comparing an econometric model
against an ARIMA, for the first time, Nelson (1972) evaluated
the predictive performance of the Federal Reserve Board-MIT-Pennsylvania (FMP) quarterly model of the U.S. economy. In
the same year Cooper compared the forecasting ability of
seven quarterly models of the U.S. economy against auto-regressive models. He, however, did not follow Box-Jenkins
strictly for his model development. The order of auto-regression in his model was determined on the basis of the
smallest residual variance, but with an arbitrary cut-off
point of eight quarters. Nelson was followed by Naylor et al.
(1972), Narsimham et al. (1974) and Christ (1975) in
comparing the relative performance of econometric models

against ARIMA models. All these researchers, except Christ concluded generally in favour of ARIMA forecasts (Cooper in favour of his autoregressive forecasts).

These studies, however, were confined to the econometric models of the North American economies only. To the best of my knowledge, no such studies (at least up to the time, early 1976, when I took up the investigation presented here) had been done with any of the European econometric models (except Prothero & Wallis, discussed shortly). In the present book I propose to report in detail the results of a similar investigation with the Bonn Monetary Model (BNM).

Though the works of Nelson, Cooper and others have already had their desired effects - starting a chain of thinking and re-thinking (Goldfeld (1972), McCarthy (1972), Green et al. (1972), Howrey et al. (1974), Cooper and Nelson (1975), Fair (1974), Hirsch et al. (1974) - for a survey of the performance of macroeconomic forecasts see Granger and Newbold (1977, pp. 289-302)), nevertheless, the results of similar exercises with econometric models of different economies should be brought to light to the added benefit of the researchers.

Commenting on Prothero and Wallis (1976), they, with the example of Hendry's (1974) eight-equation econometric model of aggregate demands in U.K., discussed the pitfalls in developing the ARIMA models, showed the relation between the econometric final equation and ARIMA, and finally came to the conclusion that in terms of 'Goodness of Fit', the econometric models performed better than the ARIMA models. They, however, did not compare the forecasting performance within the fit period and could not do so outside the fit period because of paucity of their data base. Thus, their work failed to contradict, on a justifiable ground, Nelson and Cooper (see the discussions on Prothero and Wallis (1976)).

Following Nelson, a general procedure for the investigation aiming at econometric model evaluation may be as follows:

(i) Select a number of endogenous variables, preferably, a mixture of real sector variables (GNP, state and local government expenditures, consumers' expenditures on durables and non-durables, expenditures on producers' structures and producers' durables), monetary variables (like saving deposits, short-term interest rates, yields on bonds and shares), balance-of-payments and trade sector variables (like exports, imports, in-flows and out-flows of capitals).

(ii) Develop an ARIMA model for each one of the selected variables by following an iterative cycle of identification, fitting and diagnostic checking. Care should be taken to see that the development of an ARIMA model is based on the same set of historical data of the endogenous variable, which has been used for estimating the parameters of the corresponding econometric model. In other words the sample or fit period for the ARIMA model and the econometric model should be the same.

(iii) Mark a post-sample or forecasting period of reasonable length with known realizations.

(iv) Once an appropriate ARIMA model has been developed, calculate minimum mean-square-error lead 1 forecasts for the sample and post-sample periods.

(v) Obtain another set of lead 1 sample and post-sample forecasts for each one of the selected endogenous variables by using the simultaneous system of equations of the econometric model. Distinction should be made between the fitted value and forecast. Also it should be decided whether the econometric forecasts are to be ex-post or ex-ante. For econometric model evaluation ex-post forecasts are preferred as they are free from projection error.

(vi) Examine the quality of the two sets of forecasts, ARIMA forecasts and econometric forecasts. The forecasts should be unbiased and uncorrelated with their respective errors. Futher, the residuals should be serially uncorrelated to ensure optimal utilization of the data in developing the model.

(vii) Compare the two sets of forecasts by calculating the mean squares, mean and standard deviation of the forecast errors. The same set of statistics should be calculated separately for the sample and post-sample period so as to assess the deterioration in quality of the respective forecasts.

(viii) Compare the two sets of forecasts analytically by calculating Bates-Granger (1969) composite forecasts. The argument followed here is that as the information set exploited by the econometric model includes the information set exploited by the ARIMA model the latter should not contribute significantly in the optimal combination of forecasts. In terms of Granger-Newbold (1977) concept of conditional efficiency this means that the variance of the composite forecasts should not be significantly less than the variance of the econometric forecast errors. Otherwise, the econometric model would be taken to be less efficient than its competitor, in the present case ARIMA.

For the present investigation, I could not study a mixture of endogenous variables selected from different sectors of the Bonn econometric model of Germany economy. My study had to be confined to monetary variables only, because only the monetary sector model was fitted to a longer data base of quarterly observations, sufficient for the accompanying time series analysis. The other sector models were fitted to shorter series consisting of annual observations. Thus, though I started with the aim of evaluating the Bonn econometric model of German economy what I actually, of necessity, accomplished was the evaluation of the Bonn Monetary Model (BNM) only.

My conclusion, once again, corroborated the findings of the earlier researchers, i.e., within the sample period the econometric forecasts are more accurate while outside the sample period ARIMA outperforms the econometric model.

Unlike previous researchers, I extended my investigation to study, in a limited way, the causal relationships (causality-Granger's definition) between the selected monetary variables. The statistics used for detecting and assessing causality were cross-correlations between ARIMA residuals (Pierce (1977), Pierce and Haugh (1975)). Since we fitted a univariate ARIMA model to each of the selected series, such a study of causal relationships turned out as a by-product of the main investigation. Pair-wise cross-correlations, across the selected variables, were calculated and probable causal relationships, based on Pierce's broad test (Pierce (1977)), were schematically indicated. It was expected that this study of causal relationships would bring in further insight into the forces working in the monetary system and would help to make a more effective specification of the monetary model.

For one monetary variable, short-term interest rate, I carried finer analysis (progressive χ^2-test, Feige and Pearce (1974, 1976), Layton (1978)) and discussed the consistency and usefulness of Granger's causality in examining the corresponding econometric model specification. Incidentally, I noted that money, currency in circulation and demand deposits, is determined by, not a determinant of, short-term interest rate . This appears to be contrary to what Pierce reported earlier (1977).

2. BONN ECONOMETRIC MODEL OF GERMAN ECONOMY

The Bonn econometric model of German economy is one of the important constituent models of the Project LINK (Ball, 1973). This model is exogenously connected with the Wharton School model of the U.S. economy and the London Graduate School of Business Studies model of the British economy.

The Bonn model consists of four parts; real-sector model, foreign-trade model, monetary model and balance-of-payments model. The model was initially designed in 1968 under the guidance of Professor Dr Wilhelm Krelle in the Institute for Econometrics and Operations Research, University of Bonn. Since then, the model underwent almost yearly revision. We are concerned in the present investigation with the latest version of the model, revised in 1975.

Partly due to historical reason and partly by choice the different parts of the Bonn model are made to differ in their data base. The real-sector, foreign-trade and balance-of-payments models are fitted to annual data, 1960-1970, while the monetary model is fitted to quarterly data, 44 observations in all, 1960-01 through 1970-04. It is understood that the choice for this discrepancy lies in the fact that the real-sector, foreign-trade and balance-of-payments models are supposed to provide guidance for long-range strategic decisions while the monetary model is to provide short-range tactical decisions. However, for the sake of getting a larger volume of data the present case study had to be necessarily confined to the equations of the monetary model only. The reason is that the time series analysis is essentially a large-sample exercise.

As has been mentioned earlier, the monetary model was fitted to a series of length 44, 1960-01 through 1970-04. However, at the time of the present study, the processed data (aggregated or corrected from the published data as per definition of the variables) were available for a longer period, 56 quarterly observations, 1957-01 through 1970-04, for each of the endogenous monetary variables. This length of the series was taken to be an acceptable minimum to base the associated time series analysis. The fit length of the monetary model (econometric model) was however kept unchanged at 44 quarterly observations, 1960-01 through 1970-04. However, this brought a few limitations to the present study with which this book is concerned. Firstly, the information set used by the econometric model did not completely cover the information set exploited by the subsequently developed ARIMA models. Secondly, the number of econometric forecasts was smaller than the number of ARIMA forecasts. In fact, for the sample period there were 40 econometric forecasts, 1961-01 through 1970-04 as against 50 or more ARIMA forecasts, the number of ARIMA forecasts varying depending on the structure of the model fitted. However, for both BNM and ARIMA, the length of the post-sample period was kept the same, 16 time points, 1971-01 through 1974-04.

The following sections of the book discuss the results of evaluating the predictive performance of the Bonn monetary model (BNM).

3. ARIMA MODELS FOR FIFTEEN ENDOGENOUS VARIABLES OF THE BNM MODEL

At the suggestion of the author of the BNM model, fifteen endogenous variables were selected for the present study. These include various kinds of deposits, domestic loans and open market securities held by banks, free liquid reserves and liquidity ratio of banks, money (currency in circulation plus demand deposits), two types of interest rates and yields on officially quoted bonds and shares. These are listed in Table 1 along with BNM abbreviations given within brackets.

Parsimonious ARIMA models were then developed to get an adequate representation for each one of the series (fit length 56; 1957-01 to 1970-04). The details of model identification, fitting and diagnostic checking along with graphic representation of the data are given in an appendix to this book. The fitted models along with the diagnostic test results are displayed in Table 1. For stationarity, a minimum variance was the criterion for deciding optimum differencing. Logarithmic transformation was not found necessary in any case. This may be due to the fact that the series under study were not long enough to have significant heterogeneity. Since the series consisted of seasonally unadjusted data, the seasonality had to be taken account of by seasonal differencing or by seasonal moving average parameters or by both in eigth of fifteen cases. Only in once case, 90-day money rate Frankfurt (short-term interest rate) seasonal mean adjustment was used. The remaining six series did not show any seasonality. They are open market securities (ABOM), free liquid reserves of banks (BFLR), loans to banks held by Bundesbank (PBREF), interest rate on current account loan (RKONT), yields on bonds and shares (ROBLD and RAKT). The constant term, wherever necessary, was retained whether significant or not.

None of the fitted models is a pure autoregressive or moving average model. Of the fifteen models, three are multiplicative seasonal models, one is an additive seasonal model, three are noisy random walk models and the remaining eight are various other types of ARIMA models. Except two cases, the number of parameters, leaving the constant term, is not more than two.

The serial correlations of the residuals (the first four are given in Table 2) are generally small. Box-Pierce χ^2-test was in each case based on lags 1-12. The test was insignificant in all cases, though the actual values were large (but not large enough to cause serious suspicion, Davies et al. (1977)) in two cases. No significant pattern in residual serial correlations was left unexplained in developing the models.

Table 1. ARIMA models for fifteen endogenous variables of BNM model.

Endogenous variable (BNM abbreviation)	ARIMA model	$\hat{\sigma}_a$	B-Pχ^2	(k)
Saving deposits in banks (PBDSP)	$(1-B)(1-B^4)z_t = .27 + (1 + .62B)a_t$	.63	4.49	(10)
Bundesbank deposits held by banks (ABGU)	$(1 - .50B^4)(1-B)z_t = .18 + a_t$	1.37	3.72	(10)
Domestic loans, other than Bundesbank deposits, held by banks (ABKS)	$(1-B)^2 z_t = .17 + (1 - .19B + .31B^4)a_t$	1.01	3.92	(9)
Domestic commercial bills held by banks (ABKW)	$(1-B)z_t = .41 + (1 + .56B + .51B^4)a_t$	.45	13.79	(9)
Open market securities held by banks (ABOM)	$(1 - .54B)(1-B)z_t = a_t$	.82	12.19	(11)
Free liquid reserves of banks (BFLR)	$(1 - .32B - .12B^2)(1-B)z_t = .19 + a_t$	2.57	8.3	(9)
Money (currency & demand deposits) (BGM1)	$(1-B)(1-B^4)z_t = .05 + (1 + .31B)(1 - .30B^4)a_t$	.77	6.10	(10)
Liquidity Ratio (BLQ)	$(1 - .49B)(1-B)z_t = (1 + .20B^4 + .08B^8)a_t$	.08	6.22	(9)
Loans to banks held by Bundesbank (PBREF)	$(1-B)z_t = .28 + (1 + .43B)a_t$	1.13	4.19	(10)
90-day-money-rate Frankfurt (RFFM)	$(1-B)z_t - \hat{\alpha}_t = (1 + .22B - .44B^3 - .24B^6 - .32B^9)a_t$	.68	6.67	(8)
Interest rate on current account loans (RKONT)	$(1-B)z_t = .02 + (1 + .34B)a_t$	.51	5.75	(10)

Table 1 continued.

Endogenous variable (BNM abbreviation)	ARIMA model	$\hat{\sigma}_a$	B-Pχ^2	(k)
Yield on officially quoted bonds (ROBLD)	$(1-B)Z_t = .05 + (1 + .44B)a_t$	.21	5.80	(10)
Yield on officially quoted shares (RAKT)	$(1-B)^2 Z_t = (1 - .47B)a_t$	.27	6.28	(11)
Demand deposits in banks (PBDSI)	$(1-B)(1-B^4)Z_t = .04 + (1 + .27B)(1 - .39B^4)a_t$	.72	6.41	(9)
Time deposits in banks (PBDTE)	$(1-B)(1-B^4)Z_t = .11 + (1 + .27B)(1 - .60B^4)a_t$	1.13	9.10	(9)

B is the backward shift operator; $BZ_t = Z_{t-1}$, $B^4 Z_t = Z_{t-4}$.

B-Pχ^2 (k) = Box-Pierce χ^2 with k degrees of freedom. None of the χ^2 tests is significant.

$\hat{\sigma}_a$ = standard deviation of the residuals. Variables 1-7, 9, 14 and 15 are in billions of current Deutsche marks. Variable 8 is in decimal points and variables 10-13 are in percentage points. Variable 10, 90-day-money-rate-Frankfurt, was modelled after seasonal mean adjustment.

4. ANALYSIS OF SAMPLE PERIOD LEAD 1 FORECAST ERRORS

As has been mentioned earlier, BNM was fitted to 44 quarterly observations, 1960-01 through 1970-04, while ARIMA to 56 observations, 1957-01 through 1970-04. The post-sample data for both the models consisted of 16 observations, 1971-01 through 1974-04. Lead 1 forecasts were calculated from the fitted econometric as well as ARIMA models (econometric forecasts were in fact provided by the author of the BNM). Since both the econometric and ARIMA models required varying number of lagged observations to calculate forecasts, 40 econometric and, generally, 51 ARIMA forecasts for the sample period could be obtained, while for the post sample period 16 forecasts were calculated for both the models. For some of the ARIMA's the number of within-sample forecasts was more than 51. However, to maintain uniformity, only 51 within-sample forecasts, 1958-02 through 1970-04, were considered for all the ARIMA's. The autocorrelation and cross-correlation analysis presented later was however based only on 40 observations, covering the period for which econometric forecasts were available. The analysis of sample period lead 1 forecast errors is presented in Table 2.

For the forecasts to be efficient and unbiased, lead 1 forecast error should behave as a serially independent random observation from a distribution with zero mean. In the present case, serial independence of forecast errors is more or less assured by B-Pχ^2 tests with respect to the ARIMA's. Noting that for the autocorrelations of a random series, $n \sum_1^m r(uu;k)^2 \sim \chi^2(m)$, it can be seen broadly (without adjusting for the degrees of freedom) that BNM forecast errors are not serially uncorrelated in all cases (Table 2a). χ^2 test is highly significant for domestic loans (ABKS), money (BGM1), short-term interest rate (RFFM), yields on bonds (ROBLD) and significant for domestic commercial bills (ABKW).

Serial dependence makes it difficult to test rigorously whether the mean error deviates significantly from zero or not. Bearing this in mind, it can be seen that only two means error of BNM and one mean error of ARIMA are greater than their respective standard deviation. In all other cases the mean error does not deviate significantly from zero. With the above limitation acknowledged, it can be concluded that both the sets of forecasts are generally unbiased, though the conclusion rests on a sounder basis for ARIMA forecasts than for the BNM forecasts. The significance of residual serial correlations indicates that the BNM forecasts are not all efficient.

Considering the crucial yardstick of mean squared error, it can be seen that the BNM provided generally more accurate within-sample forecasts. In three out of fifteen cases, domestic loans (ABKS), open market securities (ABOM), and money (BGM1), the ARIMA forecasts had smaller mean squared error. Except BNM forecasts of money and BNM and ARIMA forecasts of free liquid reserves (BFLR), the mean squared error are very small.

The correlations between BNM and ARIMA errors, providing a similarity between the two sets of forecasts, are substantial for many of the variables (once again rigorous testing is not valid in all cases). The highest correlations were for time deposits (PBDTE), and loans to banks held by Bundesbank (PBREF). Interestingly, for the money series the error correlation was negative and significant while it was positive for all other variables. Noticeably, BNM forecasts of money were comparatively much less accurate. The lowest error correlation was for liquidity ratio (BLQ).

Summing up, BNM and ARIMA forecasts were found to be generally unbiased, and erring in the same direction except money series. BNM forecasts had generally performed better than ARIMA forecasts except in the cases of domestic loans, open market securities and money (currency in circulation plus demand deposits) where ARIMA forecasts were found to be more accurate.

Table 2. Analysis of sample-period lead 1 forecast errors

ARIMA model: sample-period 1957-01 through 1970-04
BNM model : sample-period 1960-01 through 1970-04

Endogenous variable	BNM model errors			ARIMA model errors			Correlation between BNM and ARIMA model error
	MSE	MEAN	S.D.	MSE	MEAN	S.D.	
PBDSP	.199	-.078	.441	.381	.001	.617	.678
ABGU	.462	.007	.682	1.503	-.111	1.221	.350
ABKS	1.137	-.262	1.031	.973	.001	.986	.679
ABKW	.168	-.007	.431	.189	-.007	.435	.601
ABOM	.764	-.007	.872	.635	.000	.797	.636
BFLR	4.322	-.010	2.083	6.199	.000	2.490	.625
BGM1	3.630	.090	1.901	.572	.048	.755	-.314
BLQ	.00004	.0001	.006	.0001	.000	.008	.824
PBREF	.776	.031	.863	1.235	-.005	1.111	.709
RFFM	.131	.0001	.362	.399	-.059	.628	.433
RKONT	.154	.172	.352	.247	-.0002	.497	.645
ROBLD	.024	.002	.153	.041	.001	.202	.635
RAKT	.034	.001	.182	.070	-.003	.265	.566
PBDSI	.162	-.001	.403	.499	.062	.704	.595
PBDTE	.778	.015	.883	1.266	.211	1.105	.828

$\sqrt{40} = 6.32; \sqrt{51} = 7.14$

Table (2a). Analysis of sample-period lead 1 forecast errors (continued).

	Correlation between forecasts and errors		Serial correlation coefficients of forecast errors							
			BNM				ARIMA			
	BNM	ARIMA	r_1	r_2	r_3	r_4	r_1	r_2	r_3	r_4
PBDSP	.031	-.113	.09	-.03	-.11	-.02	.03	.04	-.06	-.14
ABGU	-.311	.218	.06	.21	.13	.07	.09	.05	-.01	.05
ABKS	.078	-.023	.18	-.47	-.17	.23	.08	.00	-.06	-.02
ABKW	-.070	-.017	.17	-.45	-.24	.10	-.08	-.08	-.04	.04
ABOM	-.113	-.013	.26	.17	.08	.22	.07	-.11	-.01	.17
BFLR	.028	-.014	.11	.00	.21	.30	.02	.05	-.14	-.14
BGM1	-.094	.001	.13	-.10	.01	.12	.01	.00	-.08	-.02
BLQ	.076	.008	.23	.10	.30	.27	.01	-.05	-.02	.00
PBREF	.078	-.032	.04	-.44	.19	.01	-.01	-.05	-.09	.14
RFFM	.001	-.156	-.22	.53	-.21	.43	.05	.07	-.01	-.02
RKONT	.048	-.234	.04	.05	.15	-.12	.03	.11	.06	-.12
ROBLD	-.003	-.039	.35	-.33	-.36	.02	.06	.07	-.10	.08
RAKT	.014	-.036	.15	.08	.10	-.19	.00	-.08	.15	.09
PBDSI	.039	.145	.05	-.26	.13	-.19	-.03	-.11	-.02	-.02
PBDTE	.062	.085	-.09	-.13	.00	.09	.02	.08	.10	.13

5. BATES-GRANGER COMPOSITE FORECAST AND ITS APPLICATION IN EVALUATING ECONOMETRIC MODEL

The principle of combining individual forecasts into a composite forecast was originally introduced by Bates and Granger (1969). Extending the use of forecast combination, Granger and Newbold (1973) later introduced their concept of "conditional efficiency" of a forecasting model. According to them, a model is conditionally efficient with respect to its competitor, if the variance of the composite forecast error (composition of the model forecast with its competing forecast) is not significantly less than that of the model forecast error itself. In that case competing forecast is taken to possess no additional useful information.

A practical procedure for calculating conditional efficiency was considered by Nelson (1972). Following Nelson, let the linear composite forecast $c_t = \beta_1 f_{B,t} + \beta_2 f_{A,t}$, where $f_{B,t}$ and $f_{A,t}$ are lead 1 model (BNM) and ARIMA forecasts respectively and β_1 and β_2 are fixed coefficients. Thus, the actual observation $X_t = \beta_1 f_{B,t} + \beta_2 f_{A,t} + e_t$, where e_t is the composite prediction error. Further if $f_{B,t}$ and $f_{A,t}$ are individually unbiased, then the composite forecast c_t will be unbiased if $\beta_1 + \beta_2 = 1$. With this assumption

$$X_t = \beta_1 f_{B,t} + \beta_2 f_{A,t} + e_t \quad \text{or} \quad (X_t - f_{A,t}) = \beta_1 (f_{B,t} - f_{A,t}) + e_t$$

The coefficient β_1 can be estimated by ordinary least squares and its difference from unity tested for significance in order to ascertain conditional efficiency of the model (BNM). As pointed out by Granger and Newbold (1977, p. 283), this procedure is to some extent deficient in the sense that it does not allow the composition weights to change through time.

In the present case study we allowed the within-sample actual realizations to regress linearly on the BNM and ARIMA lead 1 forecasts under three different schemes: (1) with a constant, (2) without a constant and (3) under the constraint $\beta_1 + \beta_2 = 1$. The results are shown in Tables 3 and 4. It can be seen that the constant term, though sometimes large, was insignificant in all cases and the estimates $\hat{\beta}_1$ and $\hat{\beta}_2$ were practically the same when the regression was done with a constant and without a constant. Besides, the weight given to the ARIMA forecast under the constraint $\beta_1 + \beta_2 = 1$ did not differ significantly from that given to the same forecast without such a restriction. These two findings led to the conclusion that the two sets of forecasts were individually unbiased and hence the composite forecast was also unbiased.

The estimates $\hat{\beta}_1$ were highly significant for all the endogenous variables; $\hat{\beta}_2$ took negative, but insignificant, values for four out of fifteen variables. For these cases, $\hat{\beta}_1$ did not differ significantly from unity and the standard error of the composite forecast was slightly larger than that of BNM forecast. We, therefore, conclude that for these four variables, namely, saving deposits (PBDSP), loans to banks held by Bundesbank (PBREF), demand deposits (PBDSI) and time deposits (PBDTE), the ARIMA forecasts contributed virtually nothing in the optimal composition and hence could be dropped from within-sample composition. The ARIMA forecasts, however, contributed significantly for six variables, namely, domestic loans (ABKS), domestic commercial bills (ABKW), open market securities (ABOM), free liquid reserves (BFLR), money (BGM1) and liquidity ratio (BLQ). They also contributed substantially, though not significantly, for Bundesbank deposits held by banks (ABGU), and yields on bonds (ROBLD) and shares (RAKT). Interestingly, for demand deposits (PBDSI), the BNM forecasts virtually eliminated ARIMA forecasts from composition, while BNM forecasts did relatively poorly in the case of money. Noting that money is equal to demand deposits plus currency in circulation, we are led to the conclusion that BNM model failed to forecast accurately the currency part of money. Another interesting point to be noted is that ARIMA forecasts contributed significantly for domestic commercial bills, free liquid reserves and liquidity ratio where the within-sample ARIMA MSE were larger than the corresponding BNM MSE. It may further be noted that the variables for which BNM forecasts performed relatively poorly are those for which BNM forecast error registered substantial serial correlations. Significant contributions from ARIMA forecasts, in addition to the presence of substantial residual serial correlations suggested that for six out of fifteen endogenous variables, BNM model underutilized the information set available to them, particularly the past history of the individual variables themselves.

The results of post-sample linear combination of the forecasts are discussed in the following section.

Table 3. **Within-sample optimal linear combination of BNM and ARIMA forecasts**

Endogenous variable	Regression with a constant		
	β_0	β_1	β_2
PBDSP	-.13 (.21)	1.05 (.15)	-.05 (.15)
ABGU	.82 (.51)	.97 (.09)	-.03 (.11)
ABKS	-.27 (.52)	.58 (.19)	.42 (.19)
ABKW	.08 (.28)	.71 (.16)	.29 (.15)
ABOM	.25 (.32)	.43 (.14)	.58 (.12)
BFLR	.56 (1.16)	.69 (.13)	.29 (.11)
BGM1	-.04 (.55)	.22 (.05)	.78 (.05)
BLQ	.00 ( )	.65 (.11)	.34 (.09)
PBREF	-.05 (.22)	1.04 (.16)	-.02 (.16)
RFFM	.01 (.17)	.98 (.10)	.02 (.09)
RKONT	.02 (.50)	.96 (.16)	.06 (.15)
ROBLD	-.02 (.23)	.83 (.16)	.18 (.16)
RAKT	.09 (.19)	.79 (.19)	.18 (.15)
PBDSI	-.07 (.30)	1.03 (.11)	-.03 (.11)
PBDTE	-.23 (.66)	1.19 (.21)	-.19 (.21)

β_0 = constant, β_1 = weight given to BNM forecast, β_2 = weight given to ARIMA forecast. The figure within the bracket is the standard error.

Table 4. **Within-sample optimal linear combination of BNM and ARIMA forecasts**

Endogenous variable	Regression without a constant (within sample)			Value of β_2 under constraint $\beta_1 + \beta_2 = 1$
	β_1	β_2	σ_e (*)	
PBDSP	1.03 (.14)	−.03 (.14)	.45 (.44)	−.01
ABGU	.91 (.08)	.09 (.08)	.68 (.68)	.09
ABKS	.56 (.20)	.44 (.20)	.99 (1.03)	.48
ABKW	.71 (.16)	.29 (.16)	.40 (.43)	.29
ABOM	.46 (.12)	.53 (.12)	.72 (.87)	.53
BFLR	.72 (.11)	.27 (.11)	1.97 (2.08)	.27
BGM1	.22 (.05)	.78 (.05)	.65 (1.90)	.78
BLQ	.67 (.09)	.33 (.09)	.01 (.01)	.33
PBREF	1.03 (.16)	−.02 (.16)	.90 (.86)	−.03
RFFM	.98 (.08)	.02 (.08)	.37 (.36)	.02
RKONT	.96 (.15)	.06 (.15)	.36 (.35)	.20
ROBLD	.83 (.16)	.17 (.16)	.16 (.15)	.17
RAKT	.85 (.14)	.15 (.14)	.19 (.18)	.15
PBDSI	1.03 (.11)	−.03 (.11)	.41 (.40)	−.03
PBDTE	1.19 (.21)	−.19 (.21)	.89 (.88)	−.17

(*) Within-sample BNM standard forecast error

6. ANALYSIS OF POST-SAMPLE LEAD 1 FORECAST ERRORS

The analysis of post-sample lead 1 forecast errors are given in Tables 5, 6 and 7. As mentioned earlier, there are sixteen time points, 1971-01 through 1974-04, in the post-sample period.

The mean squared error, mean and standard deviation of post-sample one-quarter-ahead BNM and ARIMA forecast error are given in Table 5. For BNM forecasts the exogenous variables were put at their realized values in order to avoid the error due to projection. It is clear that the accuracy of both the sets of forecasts deteriorated substantially outside the fit period. However, the MSE of ARIMA forecasts were smaller than the MSE of BNM forecasts in all cases. For domestic loans (ABKS), free liquid reserves (BFLR) and money (BGM1), the accuracy of BNM forecasts had gone down beyond expectation. No such deterioration had been recorded by the ARIMA forecasts.

For open market securities held by banks (ABOM) the BNM forecasts for quarters 1973-03 to 1974-04 were negative in sign (see Appendix). As such, probably, the corresponding BNM model for open market securities held by banks is not acceptable as a valid forecaster.

The post-sample composite forecasts were obtained in two different ways. Firstly, the post-sample BNM and ARIMA forecasts were combined into composite forecasts by using the values of $\hat{\beta}_1$ and $\hat{\beta}_2$ as obtained from the sample-period, and secondly, making the post-sample actual values to regress on the post-sample BNM and ARIMA forecasts. The MSE, MEAN

Table 5. Analysis of post-sample lead 1 forecast errors.
Post-sample period: 1971-01 through 1974-04.

Endogenous variable	BNM model errors			ARIMA model errors		
	MSE	MEAN	S.D.	MSE	MEAN	S.D.
PBDSP	9.663	-.570	3.062	7.912	.478	2.772
ABGU	44.870	-.825	6.654	14.078	-.787	3.669
ABKS	323.732	16.088	8.063	16.056	-.254	3.999
ABKW	8.576	-1.956	2.181	6.365	-.073	2.522
ABOM	39.805	2.621	5.742	1.887	.079	1.371
BFLR	398.795	9.419	17.611	86.306	.981	9.238
BGM1	156.500	6.262	10.834	6.739	.396	2.566
BLQ	.001	.010	.025	.0003	.0005	.016
PBREF	37.335	-1.691	5.873	12.433	-.410	3.502
RFFM	3.635	1.070	1.582	1.899	-.051	1.377
RKONT	.771	-.101	.871	.360	.066	.597
ROBLD	.598	.628	.451	.192	.036	.436
RAKT	.237	-.431	.234	.130	-.011	.360
PBDSI	8.560	2.151	1.986	4.882	.283	2.191
PBDTE	86.009	7.760	5.082	28.671	.880	5.282

Table 6. Analysis of the errors of post-sample composite predictions based on within-sample estimates of composition weights, β_1 and β_2.

Endogenous variable	Post-sample composite prediction error			Variance of post-sample ARIMA prediction errors
	MSE	MEAN	variance	
PBDSP	9.79	-.45	9.55	7.67
ABGU	38.45	-.68	37.95	13.47
ABKS	106.50	9.14	22.94	15.92
ABKW	5.97	-1.40	4.00	6.35
ABOM	11.23	1.26	9.67	1.88
BFLR	242.39	7.10	192.10	85.38
BGM1	17.69	1.52	15.37	6.60
BLQ	.00004	.0072	.0003	.0003
PBREF	39.46	-1.87	35.88	12.25
RFFM	3.58	1.05	2.46	1.90
RKONT	.83	-.29	.74	.36
ROBLD	.46	.52	.18	.19
RAKT	.19	-.37	.05	.13
PBDSI	8.92	2.21	4.04	4.80
PBDTE	119.23	9.16	35.28	27.88

Table 7. Post-sample optimal linear combination of BNM and ARIMA forecasts

Endogenous variable	β_1	β_2	σ_e(*)
PBDSP	.39 (.26)	.61 (.26)	2.57 (3.06)
ABGU	.12 (.15)	.86 (.15)	3.47 (6.65)
ABKS	.29 (.14)	.72 (.13)	3.47 (8.06)
ABKW	.58 (.20)	.39 (.21)	2.00 (2.18)
ABOM	-.03 (.08)	.94 (.09)	1.36 (5.74)
BFLR	.17 (.18)	.85 (.14)	8.95 (17.61)
BGM1	-.12 (.06)	1.12 (.06)	2.31 (10.83)
BLQ	.35 (.21)	.66 (.17)	.02 (.02)
PBREF	.13 (.15)	.81 (.16)	3.30 (5.87)
RFFM	.96 (.30)	.14 (.25)	1.57 (1.58)
RKONT	.06 (.24)	.94 (.24)	.60 (.87)
ROBLD	.50 (.39)	.53 (.36)	.41 (.45)
RAKT	.81 (.18)	.09 (.20)	.23 (.23)
PBDSI	.65 (.28)	.37 (.27)	1.87 (1.98)
PBDTE	.73 (.19)	.31 (.19)	3.76 (5.08)

(*) Figure within bracket is post-sample BNM standard forecast error.

and S.D. of the composite post-sample forecast errors, as obtained by the first scheme, are given in Table 6. In terms of the variance of the forecast errors, ARIMA forecasts were more accurate than the post-sample composite forecasts in eleven out of fifteen cases (Table 6).

According to the second scheme, when the actual post-sample realizations were made to regress on the post-sample BNM and ARIMA forecasts, the weight, $\hat{\beta}_2$, taken up by the latter in the process of optimal combination was significant for nine variables, large but not significant for four more variables and small and insignificant for the remaining two variables (Table 7). For six variables, $\hat{\beta}_1$ being insignificant, the composition was completely dominated by ARIMA forecasts. Invariably, the variance of the composite forecast errors was smaller than that of the BNM forecast errors when $\hat{\beta}_2$ was significantly large (Table 7).

The results discussed above indicate that the ARIMA models were generally more robust with respect to post-sample forecasts than the BNM models. Even, the post-sample ARIMA forecasts were generally more accurate than the post-sample composite forecasts based on the sample estimates of the weights.

7. CAUSAL RELATIONSHIPS BETWEEN THE SELECTED ECONOMIC VARIABLES

7.1 Granger's Definition of Causality and Its Characterization

In the previous sections of the book we developed adequate ARIMA models for each of the selected endogenous variables and compared their forecasting efficiency with that of the corresponding econometric models. We now propose to examine the causal relationships between these variables. The causal relationship to be studied is in the sense defined by Granger (1969).

Granger's definition of causality is in terms of predictability: a variable X causes another variable Y, with respect to a given universe of information set that includes X and Y, if the present Y can be better predicted by using the past values of X than by not doing so, all other information available (including past values of Y) being used in either case.

According to Granger, let $\{A_t, t = 0, \pm 1, \ldots\}$ be the given information set, including at least (X_t, Y_t).

Let
$$\bar{A}_T = \{A_s : s < T\},$$
$$\bar{\bar{A}}_T = \{A_s : s \leq T\}$$

Similarly,
$$\bar{X}_T = \{X_s : s < T\},$$
$$\bar{\bar{X}}_T = \{X_s : s \leq T\},$$
$$\bar{Y}_T = \{Y_s : s < T\}, \text{ and}$$
$$\bar{\bar{Y}}_T = \{Y_s : s \leq T\}.$$

Further, let $P_T(Y/B)$ denote the minimum MSE single-step predictor of Y given an information set B, and $\sigma^2(Y/B)$ the resulting MSE. Granger's definitions are

(i)   X causes Y :
$$\sigma^2(Y|\bar{A}) < \sigma^2(Y|\bar{A} - \bar{X}) \qquad \ldots (7.1)$$

(ii)   X causes Y instantaneously :
$$\sigma^2(Y|\bar{A}, X_T) < \sigma^2(Y|\bar{A}) \qquad \ldots (7.2)$$

Causality from Y to X is defined in the same manner. Feedback occurs if X causes Y and Y causes X.

It may be noted that the causality as defined above is not in the sense that one would usually understand, but as Granger noted (1973), it appears difficult to present an alternative definition of causality which can be tested empirically.

The problem of assessment and detection of causality between two variables was studied by Granger (1969), Sims (1972), Haugh (1976), Pierce (1977), Pierce and Haugh (1977), and Haugh and Box (1977). According to Pierce and Haugh (1977), Granger's causality can be characterized in terms of the cross-correlations between the univariate white noise innovations. They argue as follows:

A non-singular linear covariance stationary purely non-deterministic bivariate process (x_t, y_t) has the representation (Hannan 1970)

$$\begin{pmatrix} x_t \\ y_t \end{pmatrix} = (\sum_{j=0}^{\infty} \psi_j B^j) \begin{pmatrix} a_t \\ b_t \end{pmatrix}$$

$$= \psi(B) \begin{pmatrix} a_t \\ b_t \end{pmatrix} \qquad \ldots (7.3)$$

where $\{\psi_j\}$ is a sequence of 2x2 matrices,

$$x_t = T_x X_t ,$$

$$y_t = T_y Y_t ,$$

T_x and T_y are appropriate, preferably, linear, transformations; X_t and Y_t are the original untransformed variables, (a_t, b_t) is a vector of white noise sequence satisfying

$$E \begin{pmatrix} a_t \\ b_t \end{pmatrix} = \underline{0} ,$$

$$E \begin{pmatrix} a_t \\ b_t \end{pmatrix} (a_s, b_s) = \begin{cases} \Sigma \text{ (positive definite) for } t=s \\ \underline{0} \text{ for } t \neq s , \end{cases} \qquad \ldots (7.4)$$

$$\psi(B) = \sum_{j=0}^{\infty} \psi_j B^j ,$$

and B is the backward shift operator, $B^j x_t = x_{t-j}$, $B^j a_t = a_{t-j}$.

$\psi(B)$ is a matrix of polynomial in the lag operator B, convergent for $|B| \leq 1$.

It is further assumed that the above bivariate process has an equivalent autoregressive representation

$$\Pi(B) \begin{pmatrix} x_t \\ y_t \end{pmatrix} = \begin{bmatrix} A(B) & B(B) \\ C(B) & D(B) \end{bmatrix} \begin{pmatrix} x_t \\ y_t \end{pmatrix} = \begin{pmatrix} a_t \\ b_t \end{pmatrix}$$

$$\ldots (7.5)$$

where $A(B) = \sum_{j=0}^{\infty} A_j B^j$ and similarly for the other operators.

Thus for $|z| \leq 1$

$$\Pi(z) = \psi^{-1}(z) \quad \text{and} \quad |\Pi(z)| \neq 0.$$

Further, Pierce and Haugh assume that x_t and y_t each has representation as univariate linear process, which may be written as

$$\begin{bmatrix} F(B) & 0 \\ 0 & G(B) \end{bmatrix} \begin{pmatrix} x_t \\ y_t \end{pmatrix} = \begin{pmatrix} u_t \\ v_t \end{pmatrix} \qquad \ldots (7.6)$$

Thus we may derive from (7.6) a joint model of the univariate white noise which is of the form

$$\begin{bmatrix} \alpha(B) & \beta(B) \\ \gamma(B) & \delta(B) \end{bmatrix} \begin{pmatrix} u_t \\ v_t \end{pmatrix} = \begin{pmatrix} a_t \\ b_t \end{pmatrix} \qquad \ldots (7.7)$$

The various operators in these equations are connected by the relation

$$\begin{bmatrix} A(B) & B(B) \\ C(B) & D(B) \end{bmatrix} = \begin{bmatrix} \alpha(B) & \beta(B) \\ \gamma(B) & \delta(B) \end{bmatrix} \begin{bmatrix} F(B) & 0 \\ 0 & G(B) \end{bmatrix}$$

$$\ldots (7.8)$$

Pierce and Haugh then show that an analysis of (7.7) yields directly the information on the causality patterns connecting x and y (or X and Y), as u_t and v_t are the components of x_t and y_t that can not be explained from their own pasts. They thus conclude that u and v must be related inorder for x and y to be causally related. More specifically, the cross-correlations,

$$\rho(uv;k) = \frac{E(u_t v_{t+k})}{[E(u_t^2) E(v_t^2)]^{\frac{1}{2}}}, \qquad \ldots (7.9)$$

between the whitened or filtered series, $u_t = F(B)x_t$ and $v_t = G(B)y_t$, can be used to characterize different types of causality patterns as follows:

Relationship	Restrictions on $\rho(uv;k)$
X causes Y	$\rho(uv;k) \neq 0$ for some $\underline{k} > 0$
Y causes X	$\rho(uv;k) \neq 0$ for some $\underline{k} < 0$
Instantaneous causality	$\rho(uv;0) \neq 0$
Feedback	$\rho(uv;k) \neq 0$ for some $\underline{k} > 0$ and for some $\underline{k} < 0$
X causes Y but not instantaneously	$\rho(uv;k) \neq 0$ for some $\underline{k} > 0$ and $\rho(uv;0) = 0$
Y does not cause X	$\rho(uv;k) = 0$ for all $\underline{k} < 0$
Y does not cause X at all	$\rho(uv;k) = 0$ for all $\underline{k} \leq 0$
Unidirectional causality from X to Y	$\rho(uv;k) \neq 0$ for some $\underline{k} > 0$ and $\rho(uv;k) = 0$ for either (a) all $\underline{k} < 0$ or (b) all $k \leq 0$

Relationship	Restrictions on $\rho(uv;k)$
X and Y are related only instantaneously (if at all)	$\rho(uv;k) = 0$ for all $\underline{k} \neq 0$
X and Y are related instantaneously and in no other way	$\rho(uv;k) = 0$ for all $\underline{k} \neq 0$ and $\rho(uv;0) \neq 0$
X and Y are independent	$\rho(uv;k) = 0$ for all $\underline{k}$

It may further be noted that the bivariate model (7.5) implies the single-equation representations

$$y_t = V(B)x_t + f_t \quad \text{and}$$
$$x_t = W(B)y_t + g_t \qquad \ldots (7.10)$$

where

$$V(B) = -C(B)/D(B), \quad f = b_t/D(B),$$
$$W(B) = -B(B)/A(B), \text{ and } g_t = a_t/A(B) \qquad \ldots (7.11)$$

For u_t and v_t in (7.7)

$$v_t = v(B)u_t + f'_t \quad \text{and} \qquad \ldots (7.12a)$$
$$u_t = w(B)v_t + g'_t \qquad \ldots (7.12b)$$

where

$$v(B) = -\gamma(B)/\delta(B), \qquad f'_t = b_t/\delta(B),$$
$$w(B) = -\beta(B)/\alpha(B) \text{ and } g'_t = a_t/\alpha(B) \qquad \ldots (7.13)$$

In the above discussion of causality we assume that the information set consists of two variables X and Y only; in other words we consider causal relationships pair-wise among a selected group of variables.

7.2 Detection of Causality: Pierce's Broad Tests

Development of statistical tests for detecting causality is, however, beset with the difficulty that the white noise u and v are not observable in practice. So we can not have a sample white noise cross-correlation r(uv;k) to test a hypothesis regarding the population white noise cross-correlation ρ(uv;k), which is used to characterize various types of causal relationships. Instead, what we can compute is a univariate <u>residual</u> cross-correlation

$$\hat{r}(uv;k) = \frac{\Sigma \hat{u}_t \hat{v}_{t+k}}{[(\Sigma \hat{u}_t^2)(\Sigma \hat{v}_t^2)]^{\frac{1}{2}}} \qquad \ldots(7.14)$$

where $\{\hat{u}_t\}$ and $\{\hat{v}_t\}$ are two sets of ARMA (or ARIMA) residuals obtained after fitting appropriate ARMA (or ARIMA) models to the sampled series of x_t (or X_t) and y_t (or Y_t) respectively. And for the purpose of testing, we can at best have a finite set of residual cross-correlations $\hat{r}(uv;k)$. These are the sample statistics available to us for detecting different types of causal relationships. (Note: ρ(uv;k) is the population white noise cross-correlation; r(uv;k) is sample white noise cross-correlation and $\hat{r}$(uv;k) is sample residual cross-correlation; each at lag k. To make typing easier, we have used unconventional symbol to represent cross-correlation. Similar type of symbol is subsequently used to represent autocorrelation also.)

7.2.1 Testing the Independence of Two Series x and y: $\rho(uv;k) = 0$ for all k

Rigorous statistical tests can not be easily formulated in all cases of causality. We are, theoretically, on a surer ground only in testing the hypothesis that two series x and y are independent. The test is developed as follows:

The asymptotic distribution of a finite set of lagged cross-correlations, $\sqrt{n} \{r(xy;k)\}$, between two independent linear processes, x and y, is normal with zero mean vector and covariance matrix (for lags k and k+1)

$$\sum_{m=-\infty}^{+\infty} \rho(xx;m) \, \rho(yy;m+1) ,$$

where n is the size of the sample and $\rho(xx;m)$ is the autocorrelation of x at lag m (Hannan, 1970). Thus for two independent white noise processes, u and v, a finite set of cross-correlations, $\sqrt{n} \{r(uv;k)\}$, follows asymptotically $N(0, I)$. Haugh (1976) showed that if two linear processes, x and y, are independent and amenable to ARMA representation, $\phi(B)x_t = \theta(B) u_t$ (or alternatively $F(B)x_t = u_t$) and $\phi'(B)y_t = \theta'(B)v_t$ (or alternatively $G(B)y_t = v_t$) respectively, then a finite set of residual cross-correlations, $\sqrt{n} \{\hat{r}(uv;k)\}$, follows the same distribution, $N(0, I)$, as a finite set of white noise cross-correlations, $\sqrt{n} \{r(uv;k)\}$. The residual series $\{\hat{u}_t\}$ and $\{\hat{v}_t\}$ are obtained after fitting appropriate ARMA models to x and y series respectively.

From the above derivation it can be seen that a null hypothesis of series independence can be tested by calculating a set of residual cross-correlations and judging them individually against an asymptotic standard deviation of $1/\sqrt{n}$ (or in other words, forming individual χ^2 tests, each of degree of freedom 1, $\chi^2(1) = n\,\hat{r}(uv;k)^2$). A better, theoretically more sensitive, test procedure is to form a combined test

$$U = n \sum_{i=1}^{m} \hat{r}(uv;k_i)^2 \qquad \ldots(7.15)$$

where $k_1, k_2, \ldots, k_m$ are integers. Under the null hypothesis of series independence U follows $\chi^2(m)$. Thus the hypothesis of series independence can be tested by comparing the calculated value of U with the tabulated value of $\chi^2(m)$ at a specified level of significance.

It may further be noted that according to the formulation of U given above, we may consider any finite set of cross-correlations, all at positive lags, all at negative lags, consecutive or dispersed, to construct the test statistic. But as followed by Pierce (1977), a sensible approach in a situation where no specific direction of causality is assumed *a priori*, would be to consider a set of lags k such that $-N \leq k \leq M$. The values of N and M should be large enough to include non-negligibly non-zero observed cross-correlations. The statistic thus formulated would be

$$U = n \sum_{k=-N}^{M} \hat{r}(uv;k)^2 \qquad \ldots(7.16)$$

Under the null hypothesis of series independence $U \sim \chi^2(N+M+1)$. Thus the hypothesis that x and y are unrelated would not be rejected at significance level α if and only if

$$U < \chi_\alpha^2 (N+M+1) \qquad \ldots (7.17)$$

In practice the maximum negative and positive lags that can be considered in a particular case will be dictated by the length of the sample series. For example, with series of length, say 60, one should not calculate cross-correlations of lag more than 10 because to get a reliable estimate of a cross-correlation the effective number of pairs of observations should not be less than 50. Further, it should also be pointed out that the combined test (7.17) may sometimes in practice fail to provide convincing evidence for accepting the independence of two series. This point will be elaborated later while presenting a scheme for progressive χ^2 tests.

7.2.2 Assessment of Different Types of Causality

Case i: X causes Y: (X → Y)

H_0 : X $\not\to$ Y; $\rho(uv;k) = 0$ for all $k > 0$

H_1 : X → Y; $\rho(uv;k) \neq 0$ for some $k > 0$

Suggested test statistic

$$U_1 = n \sum_{k=1}^{M} \hat{r}(uv;k)^2 \sim \chi^2(M) \qquad \ldots (7.18)$$

Case ii: Y causes X: $(Y \to X)$

$H_0 : Y \not\to X;\quad \rho(uv;k) = 0$ for all $k < 0$

$H_1 : Y \to X;\quad \rho(uv;k) \neq 0$ for some $k < 0$

Suggested text statistic

$$U_2 = n \sum_{k=-1}^{-N} \hat{r}(uv;k)^2 \sim \chi^2(N) \qquad \ldots(7.19)$$

Case iii: Instantaneous causality: $(X \xrightarrow{0} Y)$

$H_0 : X \xrightarrow{0}\!\!\!\!/\; Y;\quad \rho(uv;0) = 0$

$H_1 : X \xrightarrow{0} Y;\quad \rho(uv;0) \neq 0$

Suggested test statistic

$$U_3 = n\, \hat{r}(uv;0)^2 \sim \chi^2(1) \qquad \ldots(7.20)$$

Distribution of U_1, U_2 and U_3 under the respective null hypothesis are not known fully though we have assumed them to be following $\chi^2(M)$, $\chi^2(N)$ and $\chi^2(1)$ respectively. In fact we can not have rigorous tests in these cases. According to Pierce (1977) we may assert at significance level α that

$$X \to Y \text{ if } U_1 > \chi^2_\alpha(M),$$
$$Y \to X \text{ if } U_2 > \chi^2_\alpha(N), \text{ and}$$
$$X \xrightarrow{0} Y \text{ if } U_3 > \chi^2_\alpha(1). \qquad (7.21)$$

with the acknowledgement that such tests may underestimate the significance i.e. fail to show significance when causality exists. Further, the null hypothesis X does not cause y at all and Y does not cause X at all may be tested by modifying U_1 and U_2 by incorporating the term $n\, \hat{r}(uv;0)^2$.

Feedback is assumed to be present if (7.18) and (7.19) are both significant.

7.2.3 Confirmation of Unidirectional Causality

Unidirectional causality from X to Y is inferred if test (7.18) is significant and (7.19) is insignificant with or without the significance of (7.20). But since these tests are not rigorously formulated we can not assert with confidence that in fact unidirectional causality exists whereas such an assertion may sometimes be needed. According to causality characterization, unidirectional causality from X to Y means $\rho(uv;k) \neq 0$ for some $k > 0$ and $\rho(uv;k) = 0$ for all $k < 0$ (or all $k \leq 0$). The difficulty of testing such a joint hypothesis has been discussed by Pierce and Haugh (1977).

According to Haugh (1977), the problem of confirming unidirectional causality can be solved by modelling $x(=T_x X)$ and $y(=T_y Y)$ as a dynamic regression. Suppose tests (7.18) and (7.19) indicate that the causality is unidirectional from X to Y. Then one can fit a member of the class of models, called Box-Jenkins dynamic models (Box and Jenkins, 1970):

$$y_t = \frac{\omega(B)}{\delta(B)} x_{t-b} + \frac{\theta(B)}{\phi(B)} e_t \qquad \ldots(7.22)$$

where
$$\omega(B) = \omega_0 - \omega_1 B - \omega_2 B^2 - \ldots - \omega_r B^r,$$
$$\delta(B) = 1 - \delta_1 B - \delta_2 B^2 - \ldots - \delta_s B^s,$$
$$\theta(B) = 1 + \theta_1 B + \theta_2 B^2 + \ldots + \theta_q B^q,$$
$$\phi(B) = 1 - \phi_1 B - \phi_2 B^2 - \ldots - \phi_p B^p$$

with $\delta(B) = 0$ having zeroes outside the unit circle. The identification of the dynamic regression model (D.R.M.) may be done either by the conventional method (Box-Jenkins, pp. 379-80, 1970) or by Haugh and Box procedure (1977). Haugh and Box procedure proceeds in two stages: (i) fitting of univariate time series models to each series, (ii) identifying a dynamic shock model of the type (7.12a) relating the two univariate innovation series. The models obtained at these two stages are then combined to identify a dynamic regression model (for details see Haugh and Box, 1977). The D.R.M. thus identified is fitted to the data to yield the series of residuals $\{\hat{e}_t\}$. The univariate residuals $\hat{u}_t$ ($\hat{F}(B)x_t = \hat{u}_t$) and the D.R.M. residuals $\hat{e}_t$ are then cross-correlated at positive lags

$$\hat{r}(ue;k) = (\sum_{t=1}^{n-k} \hat{u}_t \hat{e}_{t+k}) / [(\sum_1^n \hat{u}_t^2)(\sum_1^n \hat{e}_t^2)]^{\frac{1}{2}} ,$$

$$k = 0, 1, \ldots, T$$

to put up Pierce's test (Pierce 1972)

$$n \sum_{k=0}^{T} \hat{r}(ue;k)^2 \sim \chi^2(T-r-s) \qquad \ldots (7.23)$$

for judging the adequacy of the transfer function $\omega(B)/\delta(B)$.

Pierce and Haugh (1977) suggested that the univariate residuals $\hat{u}_t$ and the D.P.M. residual $\hat{e}_t$ might be cross-correlated at negative lags,

$$\hat{r}(ue;k) = (\sum_{t=1-k}^{n} \hat{u}_t \hat{e}_{t+k}) / [(\sum_1^n \hat{u}_t^2)(\sum_1^n \hat{e}_t^2)]^{\frac{1}{2}} ,$$

$$k = -1, -2, \ldots, -T ,$$

to put up a similar test,

$$n \sum_{k=-1}^{-T} \hat{r}(ue;k)^2 \sim \chi^2(T-r-s-1), \qquad \ldots(7.24)$$

for judging the hypothesis that the causality is unidirectional from X to Y, that is, there is no feedback from Y to X. In a similar manner unidirectional causality from Y to X may be confirmed.

7.3 Causal Relationships Between the Selected Monetary Variables of the Bonn Model

For the present case study, with a limited number of observations, 56 observations in the sample period, we fixed N=M=4, because, as explained earlier, to have a reliable estimate of an auto or cross-correlation the number of effective observations should preferably not be less than 50.

ARIMA residual cross-correlations $\hat{r}(k)$ for $k = -4$ to +4 were calculated pair-wise across the selected variables. For the sake of uniformity, all the cross-correlations were based on 51 pairs of residuals though in some cases we could have more pairs of residuals depending on the degree of differencing required to induce stationarity. These cross-correlations were examined following Pierce's broad tests outlined earlier. Only for one variable, namely, 90-day-money rate-Frankfurt, progressive χ^2 tests (to be explained in the next section) were applied.

Firstly the hypothesis of series independence was rejected if $51 \sum_{k=-4}^{k=4} \hat{r}^2(k) > \chi^2_{5\%}(9)$. If the overall χ^2 was significant then and only then we considered separately

$51 \sum_{k=-1}^{k=-4} \hat{r}^2(k)$, $51 \sum_{k=1}^{k=4} \hat{r}^2(k)$ and $51\hat{r}^2(0)$ to judge the presence of causality from Y to X, X to Y and instantaneous causality respectively. If the first two were individually significant with or without instantaneous causality, then feedback relationship was inferred between the two variables under consideration. Directions and strengths of causal relationships between the variables, as observed from the sample cross-correlations are summarised in Table 8.

Some of the salient findings of the cross-correlations analysis (Table 8) are as follows. Free liquid reserves (BFLR) of banks appears to be significantly cuased by domestic loans (ABKS) and money (BGM1) and weakly by yields on bonds (ROBLD), while saving deposits (PBDSP) and interest rates on current account loans (RKONT) are caused by free liquid reserves (BFLR). It appears that there is a strong contemporaneous relationship between BFLR and loans to banks held by Bundesbank (PBREF), while same type of relationship is weakly present between (BFLR) and Bundesbank deposits (ABGU), open market securities held by banks (ABOM) and short-term interest rates (RFFM). There seems to exist a feedback relationship between (BFLR) and domestic commercial bills held by banks (ABKW). Similarly, money (BGM1) causes strongly (BFLR) and is caused strongly by RFFM and RKONT. The fact that money (BGM1) is strongly and instantaneously related to demand deposits (PBDSI) is no wonder as the latter is a part of the former.

Table 8. Strengths and directions of causality relationships among selected monetary variables

	PBDSP	ABGU	ABKS	ABKW	ABOM	BFLR	BGM1	BLQ	PBREF	RFFM	RKONT	ROBLD	RAKT	PBDSI
ABGU	--													
ABKS	↔a	↑b												
ABKW	0a	--	0b											
ABOM	--	--	--	--										
BFLR	↑b	0a	↓a	↔b	0a									
BGM1	--	--	--	--	--	↑b								
BLQ	--	--	--	--	--	0b	--							
PBREF	↑b	↑b	↓b	↓b	↑a	0b	0a	0b						
RFFM	--	--	↓a	--	--	0a	↑a	↓b	--	0b				
PKONT	--	↑b	↔b	--	↑a	↓a	↑b	↓a	--	↔a				
ROBLD	--	↑a	--	--	--	↑a	↑a	↑a	--	0b	0b			
RAKT	--	--	--	--	--	↑b	0b	↑b	0a	--	↓a	--		
PBDSI	--	--	--	--	--	--	--	--	--	↓b	--	--	--	
PBDTE	--	--	↓a	--	--	--	--	--	↔b	--	--	--	--	--

-- Independent series; 0 Contemporaneous relationship; → Left margin variable causes top variable; ← Top variable causes left-margin variable.

a $.33 < R^2 < .42$; b $R^2 > .42$; $R^2 = \Sigma_{-4}^{4} r^2$

Loans to banks held by Bundesbank (PBREF) appears to be a very effective variable in the monetary system. It causes strongly and unidirectionally the saving deposits (PBDSP) and Bundesbank deposits (ABGU); weakly and unidirectionally the open market securities held by banks (ABOM) and contemporaneously the free liquid reserves of banks (BFLR), money (BGM1), liquidity ratio (BLQ) and demand deposits (PBDSI). In turn, it seems to be caused by domestic loans (ABKS), and domestic commercial bills held by banks (ABKW). There is probably a feed back relationship between time deposits (PBDTE) and (PBREF).

This section may be concluded with a note that many of the causal relationships presented in Table 8 may be due to the effect of a third variable (which may or may not be present in the selected group of fifteen variables) which has not been taken into consideration while investigating, pair-wise, causal relationships across the selected variables. Also the investigation was not extended to confirm unidirectional causality wherever it was found. These are the limitations of the present study of causal relationships. However, it is hoped that the information presented by such a limited study may also sometimes lead to a reappraisal of the presently accepted monetary theories and hence may lead to a more effective econometric specification.

7.4 Progressive χ^2 Tests for Detecting Causality

An analysis of an observed set of residual cross-correlations through the tests (7.16), (7.18) and (7.19) is a delicate matter. Anomalous situations may arise in practice. To clarify a few points an artificial example is created below.

Analysis of a set of cross-correlations   n=50

Lag k:	-2	-1	0	+1	+2	Remarks
$\hat{r}(k)$:	-.15	.08	.25	.24	.26	
$\chi^2(1)$:	1.13	.32	3.13	2.88	3.38	All insignificant at 5% level

(i) $\chi^2(5) = n \sum_{-2}^{+2} \hat{r}(k)^2 = 10.84$ Insignificant at 5% level

(ii) $\chi^2(4) = n \sum_{k \neq -1} \hat{r}(k)^2 = 10.52$ Significant at 5% level

Progressive χ^2 tests - Feige and Pearce

(iii) $\chi^2(5) = n \sum_{-2}^{+2} \hat{r}(k)^2 = 10.84$ Insignificant at 5% level

(iv) $\chi^2(3) = n \sum_{-1}^{+1} \hat{r}(k)^2 = 6.33$ Insignificant at 5% level

Progressive χ^2 tests - Layton

(v) $\chi^2(3) = n \sum_{-1}^{+1} \hat{r}(k)^2 = 6.33$ Insignificant at 5% level

(vi) $\chi^2(4) = n \sum_{-1}^{+2} \hat{r}(k)^2 = 9.71$ Significant at 5% level

(vii) $\chi^2(4) = n \sum_{-2}^{+1} \hat{r}(k)^2 = 7.46$ Insignificant at 5% level

(viii) $\chi^2(5) = n \sum_{-2}^{+2} \hat{r}(k)^2 = 10.84$ Insignificant at 5% level

All the cross-correlations are individually insignificant and also the over-all χ^2 test, (Test i) with D.F. 5, lags -2 to +2, is insignificant at 5% level of significance. Therefore, the suggested conclusion is that the hypothesis of series independence can not be rejected. But if the insignificantly small correlation at **lag** -1 is omitted from consideration then a χ^2 with D.F. 4 (Test ii) turns out significant at the same level of significance. And the conclusion is reversed. Obviously, the correlation at lag -1 contributed marginally to the overall χ^2, but added an extra degree of freedom. Besides, 'the particular set of lagged cross-correlations to be employed in constructing the test statistic is somewhat open to question', (Haugh, 1976). According to the documented theories, the set of correlations included in the test may be all at positive lags, all at negative lags, at consecutive lags or at dispersed lags. Therefore, Test (ii) is also a valid test for testing the hypothesis of series independence. Thus an overall test (i) may lead to the acceptance of a spurious independence.

To have a systematic scheme for examining various sub-sets, Feige and Pearce (1974) suggested the following statistic

$$n^2 \sum_{-p}^{+p} (n-|k|)^{-1} \hat{r}(k)^2 \sim \chi^2(2p+1) \qquad \ldots (7.25)$$

$$p = 1, \ldots, M.$$

Significance of any one of them would lead to the rejection of the hypothesis of series independence.

Firstly, Feige and Pearce followed a suggestion from Haugh (1976) that the variance of $\hat{r}(k)$ was better approximated by $(n-|k|)/n^2$, than by $1/n$. Secondly, formulation of their statistic assumed that the maximum positive lag considered in any case was equal to the maximum negative lag.

In the present artifically created example Feige and Pearce scheme, Tests (iii) and (iv), produced test results insignificant at 5% level.

According to Layton (1979), the maximum positive lag, M, need not be equal to the maximum negative lag, N. The values of M and N should be large enough, subject to the length of the series, to include non-negligibly non-zero cross-correlations. And a scheme of progressive testing should allow examination of as many subsets as possible. His scheme of progressive testing are as follows:

(a) X causes Y if any one of

$$n^2 \sum_{k=1}^{k=P} (n-|k|)^{-1} \hat{r}(k)^2 \sim \chi^2(P)$$

$P = 1, 2, \ldots, M$ is significant,

(b) Y causes X if any one of

$$n^2 \sum_{k=-1}^{k=-p} (n-|k|)^{-1} \hat{r}(k)^2 \sim \chi^2(p)$$

$p = 1, 2, \ldots, N$ is significant,

(c) X does not cause Y at all if none of

$$n^2 \sum_{k=0}^{k=P} (n-|k|)^{-1} \hat{r}(k)^2 \sim \chi^2(P+1)$$

P = 0, 1, 2, ..., M is significant,

(d) Y does not cause X at all if none of

$$n^2 \sum_{k=0}^{k=-p} (n-|k|)^{-1} \hat{r}(k)^2 \sim \chi^2(p+1)$$

p = 0, 1, 2, ..., N is significant,

(e) X and Y are independent if none of

$$n^2 \sum_{k=-p}^{k=P} (n-|k|)^{-1} \hat{r}(k)^2 \sim \chi^2(p+P+1)$$

p = 1, 2, ..., N; P = 1, 2, ..., M is significant ...(7.26)

and feedback is suspected if (a) and (b) both hold. The presence of unidirectional causality, X → Y or Y → X, should, however, be confirmed by developing dynamic regression model. This has already been explained earlier.

In the numerical example created earlier, Tests (v) to (viii) are constructed following the scheme outlined in (e). One of these tests is significant at 5% level of significance.

It is claimed that the progressive χ^2 tests, (a) to (e), will minimise the chance of accepting spurious independence. Further, Layton in his unpublished thesis suggested that the hypothesis of series independence should be tested last and, if and only if tests (a) to (d) are all insignificant. But such a procedure, it is suspected, may in practice bring interpretational problems. Besides, as we recorded earlier, theoretically we are on a surer ground in testing the hypothesis of series independence.

7.5 Causal Relationships Between Short-Term Interest Rate, 90-Day Money Rate Frankfurt (RFFM) and Other Selected Variables

A finer analysis of residual cross-correlations using progressive χ^2 tests, explained earlier, was done for one variable only, namely, short-term interest rate, 90-day money rate Frankfurt. The results of the analysis were incorporated schematically in Table 8. A part of the analysis is now shown in Table 9.

Cross-correlations between short-term interest rate (RFFM) and saving deposits (PBDSP), liquidity ratio (BLQ), interest on current account loan (RKONT), money (BGM1) and yield on officially quoted bond (ROBLD) are given in Table 9.

The progressive χ^2 tests confirm more or less the results of the broad χ^2 tests (not reported). The saving deposits (PBDSP) and short-term interest rate (RFFM) appear to be causally independent. Liquidity ratio (BLQ) causes significantly short-term interest rate (RFFM) with the strongest link at lag 1 as the progressive χ^2 tests for p = 1, 2, 3 and 4 are 10.07 (*.005), 10.15 (*.01), 10.28 (*.025) and 11.06 (*.05) respectively (significance level given within bracket). There is significant contemporaneous relationship between RFFM and BLQ also. RFFM causes BLQ weakly at lag 1 only, leading to a suspicion that there is a feedback relationship between RFFM and BLQ.

Table 9. Residual cross-correlations between short-term interest rate and other selected variables

	Residual Cross-Correlations								
Lag	-4	-3	-2	-1	0	1	2	3	4
	RFFM → PBDSP					PBDSP → RFFM			
	.18	.18	.14	.15	-.06	-.18	-.20	-.06	-.18
	RFFM → BLQ					BLQ → RFFM			
	.11	-.03	-.10	-.28	-.43	-.44	.04	-.05	.12
	RFFM → RKONT					RKONT → RFFM			
	-.32	-.23	.07	.04	.51	.27	.01	.12	-.01
	RFFM → BGM1					BGM1 → RFFM			
	.07	-.18	-.34	-.25	-.10	.05	.17	.22	.21
	RFFM → ROBLD					ROBLD → RFFM			
	-.38	-.25	.12	.11	.17	.27	.07	.13	-.09

$n = 51$; $1/\sqrt{n} = .14$

Interest rate on current account loan (RKONT) causes RFFM weakly at lag 1 only. However, there is a very strong contemporaneous relationship between RKONT and RFFM. There is also a weak feedback between RKONT and RFFM as χ^2 tests calculated progressively over negative lags are .08, .34, 3.20 and 8.86 (*.10) of which the last one is significant at 10% level for 4 degrees of freedom.

Money (BGM1) does not cause short-term interest rate (RFFM) at all. But RFFM causes money (BGM1) significantly at lags 1, 2 and 3 with strongest link at lag 2 ($\chi^2(2) = 9.36$ (*.01). In the present investigation, money is demand deposits plus currentcy in circulation.

According to Pierce (1977, p. 14, Table 4 CC→TB) currency in circulation causes short-term interest rate. Therefore, our result appears to be contrary to the finding of Pierce. The unidirectionality, however, has not been confirmed.

Progressive χ^2 tests indicate a weak causality from short-term interest rate (RFFM) to yield on officially quoted bonds (ROBLD).

Equipped with these results, we can now look at the econometric (BNM) model for the short-term interest rate (RFFM). According to Bonn Monetary Model

$$RFFM = \beta_0 + \beta_1 \text{ (Seasonal Dummy 1)} + \beta_2 \text{ (Seasonal Dummy 2)}$$
$$+ \beta_3 \text{ (Seasonal Dummy 3)} + \beta_4 \text{ (RFFM)}_{-1}$$
$$+ \beta_5 \text{ RDISK (Discount rate)} + \beta_6 (BLQ_{-1} - BLQ_{-2})$$
$$+ \text{ error} \qquad \ldots (7.27)$$

Commenting on the specification of the econometric model, we first note that the inclusion of seasonal dummies and a term with lag 1 dependent variable on the right side of equation (7.27) is consistent with our ARIMA model for RFFM (Table 1) where first differences of the seasonal mean adjusted series is taken to be stationary with significant auto correlations at various lags. Secondly, we can not comment on the inclusion of current discount rate (RDISK) as an explanatory variable as discount rate is not one of the variables selected for our study. But it has been found that interest rate on current account loans (RKONT) is causally related to RFFM. And RKONT is perhaps related to RDISK. The inclusion of liquidity ratio (BLQ) is quite consistent with our causality study though our study has suggested a lag structure different from that included in equation (7.27).

The suggested econometric model, on the basis of our study, (Tables 1 and 9) is as follows:

$$\text{RFFM} - \text{RFFM}_{-1} = \beta_0 + \beta_1 (\text{Seasonal dummy 1}) + \beta_2 (\text{Seasonal dummy 2}) + \beta_3 (\text{Seasonal dummy 3})$$
$$+ \beta_4 (\text{RKONT} - \text{RKONT}_{-1}) + \beta_5 (\text{BLQ} - \text{BLQ}_{-1})$$
$$+ \beta_6 (\text{BLQ}_{-1} - \text{BLQ}_{-2}) + \text{error}$$

...(7.28)

As mentioned in the introduction, this is an illustrative exercise aimed at (i) examining the consistency of Granger's causality with the monetary theory behind BNM model, and (ii) suggesting, if needed, an alternative specification following the lag structure indicated by the causality study. Whether the revised specification will lead to improved prediction can be judged after incorporating it (the revised model) into the simultaneous equation system, refitting them and calculating forecasts. This is considered beyond the scope of the present investigation.

BIBLIOGRAPHY

Ball, R.J. (ed.)(1973). <u>The International Linkage of National Economic Models</u>, North-Holland, Amsterdam.

Bhattacharyya, M.N. (1976). An Evaluation of Bonn Econometric Model via Time Series Analysis, Paper presented at the Econometric Society's European Meeting, Helsinki.

Box, G.E.P. and Cox, D.R. (1964). An Analysis of Transformations, <u>Journal of the Royal Statistical Society</u>, B, <u>26</u>, 211-243.

_____ and Jenkins, G.M. (1970). <u>Time Series Analysis, Forecasting and Control</u>, Holden-Day, San Francisco.

_____ and Pierce, D.A. (1970). Distribution of Residual Autocorrelations in Autoregressive-Integrated Moving Average Time Series Models, <u>Journal of the American Statistical Association</u>, <u>65</u>, 1509-1526.

_____ and MacGregor, J.F. (1974). The Analysis of Closed-Loop Dynamic Stochastic Systems, <u>Technometrics</u>, <u>16</u>, 391-398.

Caines, P.E. and Chan, C.W. (1975). Feedback between Stationary Stochastic Processes, <u>IEEE Transaction On Automatic Control</u>, AC-20, 498-508.

Chatfield, C. and Prothero, D.L. (1973). Box Jenkins Seasonal Forecasting: Problems in a Case Study (with discussions), <u>Journal of the Royal Statistical Society</u>, <u>A</u>, 136, 295-315.

Christ, C.F. (1975). Judging the Performance of the Econometric Models of the U.S. Economy, *International Economic Review*, 16, 54-74.

Cooper, R.L. (1972). The Predictive Performance of Quarterly Econometric Models of the United States, in Hickman, B.G. (ed.), *Econometric Models of Cyclical Behaviour*, Columbia University Press, New York.

Cooper, J.P. and Nelson, C.R. (1975). The ex-ante Prediction Performance of the St. Louis and F.R.B.-M.I.T.-Penn. Econometric Models and some results on Composite Predictors, *Journal of Money Credit and Banking*, 7, 1-32.

Cramer, R.H. and Miller, R.B. (1974). Dynamic Modelling and Multivariate Time Series for Use in Bank Analysis, Mimeographed, Graduate School of Business, University of Wisconsin.

Davies, N., Triggs, C.M. and Newbold, P. (1977). Significance levels of the Box-Pierce portmanteau statistic in finite samples, *Biometrika*, 64, 517-522.

De Reyes, F. (1974). A Test for the Direction of Causality between Money and Income in Canada, Japan and United States, Ph.D. Dissertation, Department of Economics, Iowa State University.

Fair, R.C. (1974). An Evaluation of a Short-run Forecasting Model, *International Economic Review*, 15, 285-303.

Feige, E.L. and Pearce, D.K. (1974). The Causality Relationship between Money and Income: A Time Series Approach, Paper presented at the Annual Meeting of the Midwest Economic Association, Chicago.

Goldfeld, S.M. (1972). Discussion of paper by R.L. Cooper, in Hickman, B.G. (ed.), Econometric Models of Cyclical Behaviour, Columbia University Press, New York.

Granger, C.W.J. (1963). Economic Processes Involving Feedback, Information and Control, 6, 28-48.

_____ (1969). Investigating Causal Relations by Econometric Models and Cross-Spectral Methods, Econometrica, 37, 424-438.

_____ (1972). Time Series Modelling and Interpretation, Paper presented at European Economic Congress, Budapest.

_____ (1973). Causality, Model Building and Control: Some Comments, Paper presented at the I.F.A.C./I.F.O.R.S. International Conference on Dynamic Modelling and Control, University of Warwick, Coventry, England.

_____ and Newbold, P. (1973). Some Comments on the Evaluation of Economic Forecasts, Applied Economics, 5, 35-47.

_____ (1974). Spurious Regressions in Econometrics, Journal of Econometrics, 2, 111-120.

Granger, C.W.J. and Newbold, P. (1975). Economic Forecasting: the atheist's view point, in Renton, G.A. (ed.), *Modelling the Economy*, Heinemann, London.

Granger, C.W.J. (1976). Identification of Two-Way Causal Systems, in Intriligator, M.D. (ed.), *Frontiers of Quantitative Economics*, Vol. 3, North-Holland, Amsterdam.

_____ (1977). Comments on "Relationship - and the Lack thereof ...", by David Pierce, *Journal of the American Statistical Association*, 72, 22-23.

_____ and Newbold, P. (1977). *Forecasting Economic Time Series*, Academic Press, New York.

Green, G.R., Liebenberg, M. and Hirsch, A.A. (1972). Comment on paper by R.L. Cooper, in Hickman, B.G. (ed.), *Econometric Models of Cyclical Behaviour*, Columbia University Press, New York.

Hannan, E.J. (1963). Regression in Time Series, in Rosenblatt, M. (ed.), *Time Series Analysis*, Wiley, New York.

_____ (1970). *Multiple Time Series*, Wiley, New York.

Haugh, L.D. (1972). The Identification of Time Series Interrelationships with special reference to Dynamic Regression Models, unpublished Ph.D. Dissertation, Department of Statistics, University of Wisconsin.

_____ (1976). Checking the Independence of Two Covariance-Stationary Time Series: A Univariate Residual Cross-Correlation Approach, *Journal of the American Statistical Association*, 71, 378-385.

Haugh, L.D. and Box, G.E.P. (1977). Identification of Dynamic Regression (Distributed lag) Models Connecting two Time Series, *Journal of the American Statistical Association*, 72, 121-130.

Hendry, D.F. (1974). Stochastic Specification in an Aggregate Demand Model of the United Kingdom, *Econometrica*, 42, 559-578.

Hirsch, A.A., Grimm, B.T. and Narasimham, G.V.L. (1974). Some Multiplier and Error Characteristics of the B.E.A. Quarterly Model, *International Economic Review*, 16, 616-631.

Howrey, E.P., Klein, L.R. and McCarthy, M.D. (1974). Notes on testing the Predictive Performance of Econometric Models, *International Economic Review*, 15, 366-383.

Klein, L.R. (1971). *An Essay on the Theory of Economic Prediction*, Markham, Chicago.

Krelle, W. et.al. (1969). *Ein Prognosesystem für die Wirtschaftliche Entwicklung der Bundesrepublik Deutschland*, Meisenheim, Verlag Anton Hain.

Layton, A.P. (1978). A Time Series Analysis of the Causality Relations between Money, Price and Income in Australia, unpublished Masters Thesis, Department of Economics, University of Queensland.

Ljung, G.M. and Box, G.E.P. (1976). A modification of the overall χ^2 test for Lack of fit in Time Series Models, Technical Report No. 477, Department of Statistics, University of Wisconsin.

Ljung, G.M. and Box, G.E.P. (1978). On a Measure of Lack of Fit in Time Series Models, Biometrika, 65, 297-303.

Martiensen, J. (1975). Ein Okonometrisches Vierteljahresmodell des Geldund-Kreditsectors für die Bundesrepublik Deutschland, Meisenheim, Verlag Anton Hain.

McCarthy, M.D. (1972). Discussion of paper by R.L. Cooper, in Hickman, B.G. (ed.), Econometric Models of Cyclical Behaviour, Columbia University Press, New York.

Narasimham, G.V.L. and Singpurwalla, N.D. (1974). Comparison of Box-Jenkins and BEA Quarterly Econometric Model Predictive Performance, Proceedings of the American Statistical Association, Business and Economic Statistics Section, Washington D.C., 501-504.

Naylor, T.H., Sears, T.G. and Wichern, D.W. (1972). Box-Jenkins Models: An Alternative to Econometric Models, International Statistical Review, 40, 123-139.

Nelson, C.R. (1972). The Prediction Performance of the FRB-MIT-PENN Model of the U.S. Economy, American Economic Review, 62, 902-917.

Newbold, P. and Granger, C.W.J. (1974). Experience with Forecasting Univariate Time Series and Combination of Forecasts, Journal of the Royal Statistical Society, A, 137, 131-146.

Pierce, D.A. (1971). Least Squares Estimation in the Regression Model with ARIMA errors, Biometrika, 58, 299-312.

Pierce, D.A. (1971). Distribution of Residual Autocorrelations in the Regression Model with Autoregressive Moving Average Errors, Journal of the Royal Statistical Society, B, 33, 140-146.

_____ (1972). Least Squares Estimation in Dynamic-Disturbance Time Series Models, Biometrika, 59, 73-78.

_____ (1972). Residual Correlations and Diagnostic Checking in Dynamic-Disturbance Time Series Models, Journal of the American Statistical Association, 67, 636-640.

_____ (1975). Forecasting in Dynamic Models with Stochastic Regressors, Journal of Econometrics, 3, 349-374.

_____ (1979). R^2 Measures for Time Series, Journal of the American Statistical Association, (to appear).

_____ (1977). Relationships - and the Lack Thereof - Between Economic Time Series with Special Reference to Money and Interest Rates (with discussions), Journal of the American Statistical Association, 72, 11-26.

_____ and Haugh, L.D. (1977). Causality in Temporal Systems: Characterization and a Survey, Journal of Econometrics, 5, 265-293.

Prothero, D.L. and Wallis, K.F. (1976). Modelling Macroeconomic Time Series (with discussions), Journal of the Royal Statistical Society, A, 139, 468-500.

Sims, Christopher A. (1972). Money, Income and Causality, <u>American Economic Review</u>, <u>62</u>, 540-552.

Stekler, H.O. (1968). Forecasting with Econometric Models: An Evaluation, <u>Econometrica</u>, <u>36</u>, 437-463.

Theil, H. (1961). <u>Economic Forecasts and Policy</u>, North-Holland, Amsterdam.

Wall, K.D., Preston, A.J., Bray, J.W. and Peston, M.H. (1975). Estimates of a Simple Control Model of the U.K. Economy, in Renton, G.A. (ed.), <u>Modelling the Economy</u>, Heinemann, London.

Zeller, S.H. and Pierce, D.A. (1973). ARIMA forecasting of the Monetary Aggregates: A Preliminary Examination, Mimeographed, Federal Reserve Board, Washington D.C..

Zellner, A. and Palm, F. (1974). Time Series Analysis and Simultaneous Equation Econometric Models, <u>Journal of Econometrics</u>, <u>2</u>, 17-54.

APPENDIX

Development of ARIMA models, autoregressive-integrated-moving average models, - model identification, fitting and diagnostic checking, for the selected endogenous variables of the Bonn Monetary Model, sample period 1957-01 through 1970-04, are given in this appendix. Also, post-sample, 1971-01 through 1974-04, econometric, ARIMA and composite forecasts are compared with actual realizations.

Series 1: Saving deposits in banks (PBDSP) in billions of Deutsche Marks

year	Quarter			
	1	2	3	4
1957	25.91	26.92	27.67	29.12
1958	31.46	32.91	34.32	36.04
1959	38.61	40.38	42.00	44.17
1960	46.73	48.33	49.72	51.80
1961	55.05	56.33	57.58	59.32
1962	62.76	64.60	65.99	68.06
1963	72.40	74.33	76.35	79.33
1964	84.02	86.22	88.29	91.49
1965	97.21	100.60	103.27	107.14
1966	113.05	115.71	118.67	122.83
1967	129.77	132.73	135.40	140.39
1968	148.88	152.44	156.00	161.82
1969	170.80	174.75	178.40	183.34
1970	190.81	192.78	194.65	201.41
1971	213.01	217.49	221.20	229.15
1972	243.06	250.03	256.25	267.76
1973	275.64	276.16	274.36	283.20
1974	298.86	301.78	305.44	317.85

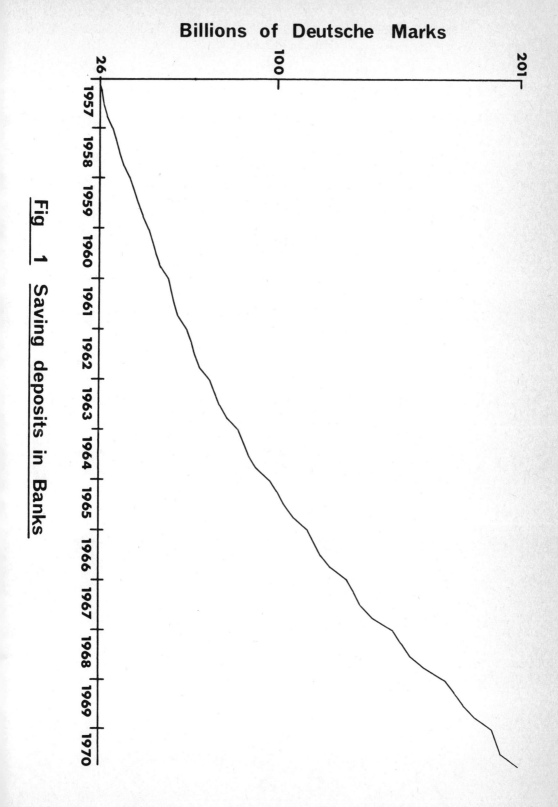

Fig. 1 Saving deposits in Banks

Sample autocorrelations and partial autocorrelations
(saving deposits)

	Lag	Autocorrelations				Partial autocorrelations			
z_t	1 - 4	.95	.89	.84	.78	.95	-.02	-.05	-.05
	5 - 8	.72	.66	.61	.55	-.02	-.03	-.04	-.04
	9 -12	.50	.45	.40	.35	-.01	-.02	-.03	-.04
		Mean = 94.13				var = 2755			
$\nabla_1 z_t$	1 - 4	.37	.07	.41	.81	.37	-.07	.48	.71
	5 - 8	.27	.02	.33	.65	-.11	-.19	-.25	.08
	9 -12	.16	-.05	.24	.49	-.05	-.00	-.06	-.01
		Mean = 3.19				var = 3.66			
$\nabla_1^2 z_t$	1 - 4	-.22	-.53	-.12	.81	-.22	-.61	-.74	.32
	5 - 8	-.21	-.48	-.08	.72	-.05	-.07	-.27	-.06
	9 -12	-.20	-.42	-.03	.61	-.11	-.05	-.04	-.12
		Mean = 0.11				var = 4.39			
$\nabla_s z_t$	1 - 4	.96	.92	.87	.82	.96	-.03	-.12	-.14
	5 - 8	.15	.69	.62	.56	-.10	-.07	-.02	.04
	9 -12	.50	.45	.39	.33	-.01	-.02	-.03	-.10
		Mean = 12.89				var = 26.66			
$\nabla_1 \nabla_s z_t$	1 - 4	.43	.13	.01	.09	.43	-.06	-.02	.10
	5 - 8	-.04	-.08	-.18	-.13	.05	-.09	-.15	.00
	9 -12	-.15	-.14	.11	.08	-.09	-.06	.22	-.07
		Mean = .25				var = .5029			

Model identification:

The autocorrelations of the undifferenced (original) series persist significantly at higher lags and the partial autocorrelation is very high (nearly one) at lag 1 and insignificant afterwards. This indicates that there is trend in the data and, therefore, differencing is needed. The first-differenced series shows the presence of strong seasonality - the autocorrelation function having positive peaks at lags 4, 8 and 12. A second differencing does not remove seasonality from the data. With a seasonal differencing ($\nabla_1 = 1-B^4$), the trend reappears.

A first difference of the seasonal differences appears to have induced stationarity, with no pattern in the autocorrelations. At this tage, a significant autocorrelation appears at lag 1 only. Also, a partial autocorrelation appears significant at the same lag and is insignificant afterwards. But an autoregressive scheme is ruled out as the autocorrelation function does not appear to have decayed exponentially. Further, the variability of the first difference of the seasonal differeneces is a minimum indicating that no unnecessary differencing has been done.

The tentatively identified model is

$$(1-B)(1-B^4)z_t = \theta_0 + a_t + \theta_1 a_{t-1}.$$

Fitting and diagnostic checking:

The fitted model is
$$(1-B)(1-B^4)z_t = .27 + a_t + .62a_{t-1}$$
$$(.13)$$

$$\hat{\sigma}_a = 0.63;\ \text{Box-Pierce}\ \chi^2(12-2) = 4.49$$

Corresponding econometric model:

$$\frac{PBDSP}{BGM2_{-1}} = \underset{(0.0339)}{0.0529} - \underset{(0.0013)}{0.0135}\ QS2 - \underset{(0.0012)}{0.0152}\ QS3$$

$$-\underset{(0.0019)}{0.0112}\ QS4 + \underset{(0.0601)}{0.9314}\left(\frac{PBDSP}{BGM2_{-1}}\right)_{-1}$$

$$+ \underset{(0.0023)}{0.0049}\ RSPAR - \underset{(0.0005)}{0.0020}\ RTERM$$

$$- \underset{(0.0008)}{0.0014}\ RKONT + \underset{(0.0428)}{0.0745}\ \frac{(GDPN - T)}{BGM2_{-1}}$$

$$- \underset{(2.5002)}{5.5176}\ \frac{1}{BGM2_{-1}}$$

$$DW = 1.817 \qquad R = 0.9997$$

Post-sample lead 1 ARIMA forecasts compared with actual values, BNM forecasts and composite forecasts
(Saving deposits)

		Quarter 1	Quarter 2	Quarter 3	Quarter 4
1971	Actual:	213.02	217.49	221.20	229.15
	Forecast:				
	BNM	211.27	217.60	223.27	226.96
	ARIMA	209.15	217.68	219.51	229.28
	COMPOSITE	211.22	217.48	223.25	226.77
1972	Actual:	243.06	250.03	256.25	264.76
	Forecast:				
	BNM	240.69	251.00	255.88	266.54
	ARIMA	240.94	249.72	254.58	265.51
	COMPOSITE	240.54	250.91	255.77	266.43
1973	Actual:	275.64	276.16	274.36	283.20
	Forecast:				
	BNM	277.93	281.13	281.53	281.90
	ARIMA	278.47	281.11	279.56	279.90
	COMPOSITE	277.76	280.97	281.43	280.80
1974	Actual:	298.86	301.78	305.44	317.85
	Forecast:				
	BNM	295.40	304.30	308.69	313.29
	ARIMA	296.41	301.18	300.63	317.56
	COMPOSITE	295.20	304.22	308.76	312.99

Series 2: Bundesbank deposits held by banks (ABGD) in billions of Deutsche Marks

| | Quarter | | | |
year	1	2	3	4
1957	3.78	4.68	5.15	6.28
1958	5.70	6.11	6.36	7.37
1959	6.64	6.86	6.67	8.11
1960	9.03	10.64	11.80	12.75
1961	11.45	10.48	9.45	10.05
1962	8.54	8.93	9.34	10.41
1963	9.08	9.83	10.24	11.63
1964	10.74	10.84	12.27	13.75
1965	13.08	13.22	14.05	15.41
1966	14.68	14.81	15.54	16.46
1967	14.26	13.39	11.42	13.33
1968	12.38	13.45	13.67	17.46
1969	13.85	16.99	18.95	18.09
1970	17.25	18.66	23.38	25.19
1971	26.84	28.00	33.66	33.17
1972	28.72	31.84	43.00	46.24
1973	49.79	53.11	56.33	55.76
1974	52.49	52.00	47.54	45.57

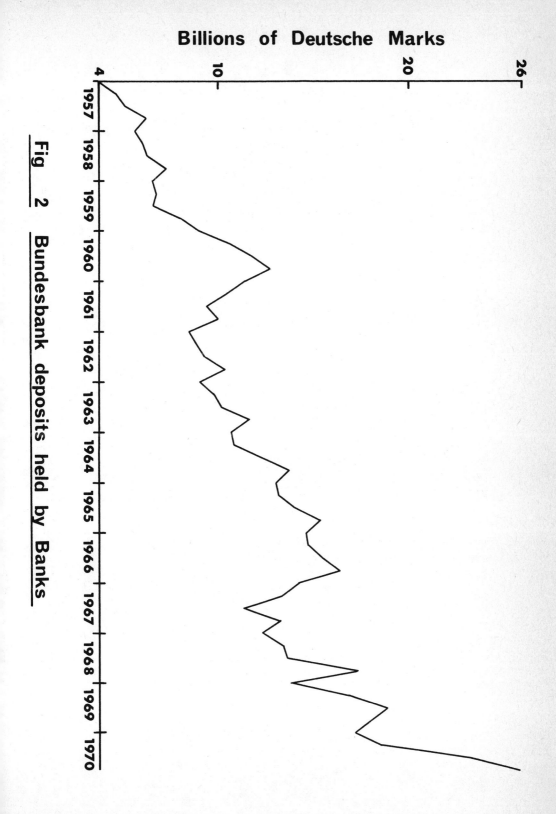

Fig 2 Bundesbank deposits held by Banks

Sample autocorrelations and partial autocorrelations
(Bundesbank deposits)

	Lag	Autocorrelations				Partial autocorrelations			
z_t	1 - 4	.83	.70	.62	.58	.83	.04	.11	.12
	5 - 8	.49	.40	.34	.34	-.15	-.03	.01	.12
	9 -12	.25	.22	.19	.19	-.21	.16	-.03	.03
		Mean = 11.87				var = 20.08			
$\nabla_1 z_t$	1 - 4	-.09	.04	-.18	.34	-.09	.03	-.18	.33
	5 - 8	-.19	-.05	-.12	.27	-.17	-.11	.00	.13
	9 -12	-.13	-.05	-.04	.16	-.06	-.06	.05	-.01
		Mean = .40				var = 2.07			
$\nabla_1^2 z_t$	1 - 4	-.59	.19	-.33	.50	-.59	-.24	-.53	.05
	5 - 8	-.34	.08	-.15	.30	.00	-.17	-.19	-.07
	9 -12	-.20	.03	.07	.25	.00	-.04	-.07	.12
		Mean = .03				var = 4.52			
$\nabla_s z_t$	1 - 4	.68	.43	.20	-.10	.68	-.06	-.13	-.31
	5 - 8	-.12	-.23	-.24	-.15	.23	-.22	.03	.01
	9 -12	-.16	-.22	-.24	-.28	-.05	-.36	.04	-.07
		Mean = 1.25				var = 5.02			
$\nabla_1 \nabla_s z_t$	1 - 4	.04	.11	.04	-.43	.04	.11	.03	-.45
	5 - 8	-.10	-.09	-.13	.06	-.08	.04	-.08	-.14
	9 -12	.21	.03	.14	-.07	.22	.01	-.04	-.16
		Mean = .12				var = 2.38			

Model Identification:

The autocorrelations of the original series indicate that there is trend in the data and those of the first differences, $(\nabla_1 z_t)$, indicate the presence of seasonality. Assuming that the seasonal difference of the first differences, $(\nabla_4 \nabla_1 z_t)$, is stationary, though its variability appears to be slightly larger than that of the first differences, the model

$$(1-B^4)(1-B)z_t = (1 - \theta B^4)a_t$$

is tentatively entertained. However, the fitted model

$$(1-B^4)(1-B)z_t = (1 - .97B^4)a_t$$

is not acceptable as the moving average operator has virtually a unit root and hence, the model is not invertible. This indicates that the seasonal differencing was perhaps unwarranted and had apparently induced significant autocorrelations at seasonal lags. Reconsidering the first differences as the basic stationary series, it may also be noted that the Random Walk model

$$(1-B)z_t = a_t$$

is not acceptable as there is a strong evidence of seasonality present in the series. Alternatively, the model

$$(1 - \phi B^4)(1-B)z_t = \theta + a_t$$

is suggested with the hope that the seasonal autoregressive operation will take care of the positive and declining autocorrelations at the seasonal lags (4, 8 and 12).

Fitting and diagnostic checking:

The fitted model is

$$(1 - .50B^4)(1-B)z_t = .18 + a_t$$
$$(.11)$$

$\hat{\sigma}_a = 1.37$; Box-Pierce $\chi^2(12-2) = 3.72$

Corresponding econometric model:

ABGU = ABEXR + SRSOL

Post-sample lead 1 ARIMA forecasts compared with the actual values, BNM forecasts and composite forecasts
(Bundesbank deposits)

		Quarter			
		1	2	3	4

1971	Actual:
	Forecast:
	  BNM
	  ARIMA
	  COMPOSITE
		26.84
		
		25.41
		25.16
		25.31
			28.00
			
			29.68
			28.26
			28.56
				33.66
				
				32.76
				32.72
				32.66
					33.17
					
					30.11
					36.28
					31.53

1972	Actual:
	Forecast:
	  BNM
	  ARIMA
	  COMPOSITE
		28.72
		
		24.54
		32.39
		25.15
			31.84
			
			32.98
			30.14
			31.72
				43.00
				
				42.64
				36.60
				41.96
					46.24
					
					50.45
					45.53
					49.86

1973	Actual:
	Forecast:
	  BNM
	  ARIMA
	  COMPOSITE
		49.79
		
		50.54
		45.36
		49.93
			53.11
			
			49.13
			51.26
			49.16
				56.33
				
				47.86
				58.07
				48.59
					55.76
					
					47.09
					58.89
					47.98

1974	Actual:
	Forecast:
	  BNM
	  ARIMA
	  COMPOSITE
		52.49
		
		53.14
		55.02
		53.13
			52.00
			
			60.88
			54.03
			60.08
				47.54
				
				59.89
				56.91
				59.44
					45.57
					
					62.15
					50.02
					60.89

Series 3: Domestic loans, other than Bundesbank deposits, held by banks (ABKS) in billions of Deutsche Marks

year	Quarter			
	1	2	3	4
1957	71.92	73.40	75.39	78.07
1958	80.77	82.97	85.60	88.88
1959	92.10	94.73	99.35	103.74
1960	107.55	111.55	115.41	119.70
1961	124.33	129.37	134.40	139.28
1962	143.72	148.51	153.86	159.21
1963	164.02	168.95	174.87	181.27
1964	187.43	192.64	198.98	205.78
1965	212.30	219.03	226.45	233.40
1966	240.74	248.22	254.00	258.27
1967	262.16	266.59	270.84	276.65
1968	283.13	291.42	299.55	309.85
1969	319.71	329.82	341.09	356.48
1970	371.18	382.48	394.69	406.87
1971	419.34	432.58	450.21	471.10
1972	488.68	509.28	528.64	554.73
1973	584.55	608.17	623.71	640.55
1974	653.43	663.97	678.01	690.47

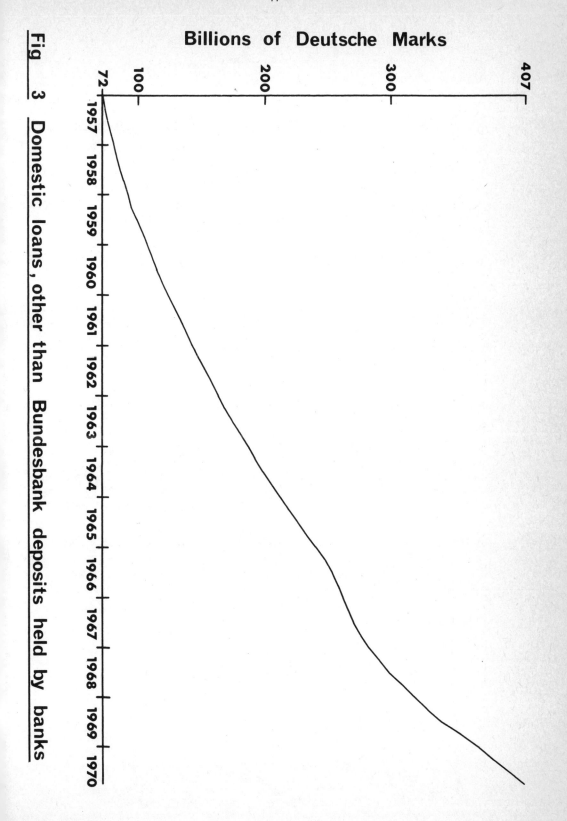

Fig 3 Domestic loans, other than Bundesbank deposits held by banks

Sample autocorrelations and partial autocorrelations
(Domestic loans)

	Lag	Autocorrelations				Partial autocorrelations			
z_t	1 - 4	.94	.88	.82	.76	.94	-.03	-.02	-.03
	5 - 8	.70	.65	.60	.55	-.01	-.01	-.02	-.02
	9 -12	.50	.45	.41	.36	-.02	-.02	-.02	-.02
		Mean = 199.0				var = 9071			
$\nabla_1 z_t$	1 - 4	.89	.77	.70	.58	.88	-.07	.13	-.25
	5 - 8	.42	.32	.26	.18	-.23	.14	.01	.05
	9 -12	.09	.07	.04	.02	-.12	.09	-.06	.12
		Mean = 6.0				var = 9.50			
$\nabla_1^2 z_t$	1 - 4	.02	-.25	-.02	.20	.02	-.25	-.01	.15
	5 - 8	-.11	-.06	.04	-.11	-.14	.03	-.01	-.17
	9 -12	-.08	-.04	.01	-.22	-.02	-.12	-.04	-.24
		Mean = .20				var = 1.08			
$\nabla_s z_t$	1 - 4	.91	.79	.66	.52	.91	-.26	-.11	-.09
	5 - 8	.39	.29	.20	.13	.02	.00	-.02	-.04
	9 -12	.07	.04	.02	.03	.02	.07	.03	.06
		Mean = 24.16				var = 124.5			
$\nabla_1 \nabla_s z_t$	1 - 4	.72	.46	.18	.02	.72	-.11	-.22	.01
	5 - 8	-.05	-.10	-.18	-.25	.04	-.08	-.20	-.06
	9 -12	-.27	-.31	-.30	-.26	.02	-.21	-.05	.01
		Mean = .81				var = 3.28			

Model identification:

This is a series which follows a steady upward trend, almost undisturbed by random fluctuations (see Fig. 3). The first differencing fails to remove the trend (see the autocorrelations and partial autocorrelations). A seasonal differencing and a first differencing of the seasonal differences seem to be unnecessary as they tend to increase the variability. Noting the significant autocorrelations of the second differences, the following model is tentatively identified.

$$(1-B)^2 z_t = \theta_0 + a_t + \theta_2 a_{t-2} + \theta_4 \dot{a}_{t-4}.$$

Fitting and diagnostic checking:

The fitted model is

$$(1-B)^2 z_t = .17 + a_t - .19 a_{t-2} + .31 a_{t-4}$$
$$(.15)(.15)$$

$\hat{\sigma}_a = 1.01$; Box-Pierce χ^2 (12-3) = 3.92

Corresponding econometric model:

$\dfrac{ABKS}{GDPT} = $ 0.1707 - 0.0182 QS2 + 0.0165 QS3 - 0.0311 QS4
$\phantom{\dfrac{ABKS}{GDPT} = }$ (0.2192) (0.0061) (0.0072) (0.0117)

 + 0.9137 $\dfrac{ABKS}{GDPT}_{-1}$ - 0.0143 RKONT - 0.0284 ROBLD
 (.0829) (0.0071) (0.0080)

 + 0.0253 RW - 12.3192 $\dfrac{1}{GDPT}_{-1}$ + 0.3308 $\dfrac{GDPN}{GDPT}$
 (0.0101) (8.1287) (0.0963)

 DW = 1.654 R = 0.9996

Post-sample lead 1 ARIMA forecasts compared with actual values, BNM forecasts and composite forecasts
(Domestic loans)

		Quarter			
		1	2	3	4
1971	Actual:	419.34	432.58	450.21	471.10
	Forecast:				
	BNM	417.82	431.40	444.24	468.98
	ARIMA	419.23	431.98	445.97	467.90
	COMPOSITE	418.23	431.44	444.78	463.80
1972	Actual:	488.68	509.28	528.64	554.73
	Forecast:				
	BNM	476.97	494.73	513.65	533.36
	ARIMA	491.38	506.00	531.81	548.53
	FORECAST	483.10	499.46	521.45	539.79
1973	Actual:	584.55	608.17	623.71	640.55
	Forecast:				
	BNM	557.77	586.21	607.92	622.92
	ARIMA	580.79	614.36	630.24	642.54
	FORECAST	567.66	598.35	617.47	631.27
1974	Actual:	653.43	663.97	678.01	690.47
	Forecast:				
	BNM	634.19	643.02	651.16	663.67
	ARIMA	660.00	664.96	673.94	691.80
	FORECAST	645.27	652.39	660.90	675.77

Series 4: Domestic commercial bills held by banks (ABKW) in billions of Deutsche Marks

year	Quarter			
	1	2	3	4
1957	13.42	13.49	13.37	13.71
1958	13.67	13.41	13.25	13.30
1959	13.55	13.98	14.16	14.65
1960	15.15	15.37	15.43	15.98
1961	16.62	17.33	17.65	18.06
1962	18.08	18.71	18.95	19.33
1963	19.37	19.98	20.04	20.50
1964	20.25	20.90	21.23	22.21
1965	22.76	23.60	24.17	24.84
1966	25.08	25.86	25.81	25.84
1967	25.35	25.34	25.66	26.69
1968	26.61	27.26	28.49	30.10
1969	30.93	31.18	32.01	34.87
1970	35.91	35.76	36.13	36.50
1971	37.25	37.03	38.00	38.86
1972	39.14	41.20	40.47	40.48
1973	35.45	30.33	29.59	29.72
1974	29.96	31.58	33.83	35.65

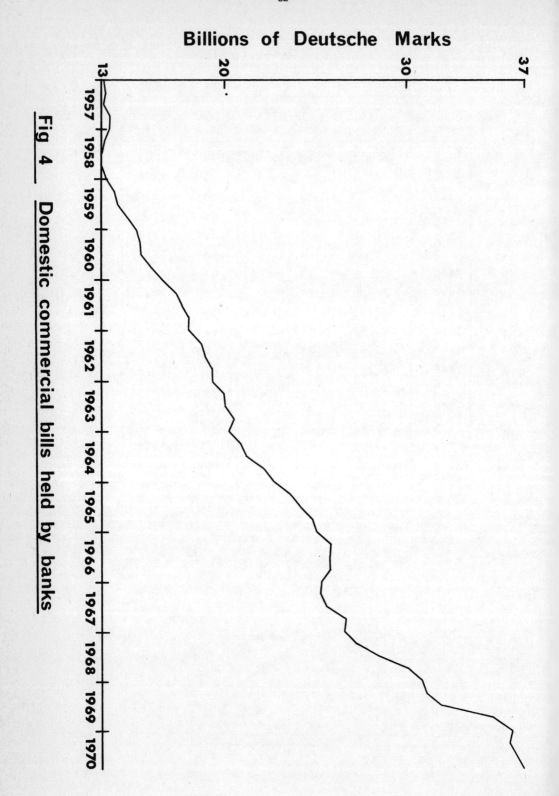

Fig 4 Domestic commercial bills held by banks

Sample autocorrelations and partial autocorrelations
(Domestic Commercial Bills)

	Lag	Autocorrelations	Partial autocorrelations
z_t	1 - 4	.94 .88 .82 .75	.94 -.06 -.05 -.07
	5 - 8	.68 .62 .57 .51	-.04 .06 -.03 -.04
	9 -12	.46 .41 .37 .34	-.03 .03 .02 .00
		Mean = 21.82	Var = 47.51
$\nabla_1 z_t$	1 - 4	.33 .08 .03 .37	.33 -.04 .01 .40
	5 - 8	.10 -.02 -.33 .03	-.20 -.01 -.37 .19
	9 -12	-.09 -.07 -.24 .01	-.23 .07 .03 .01
		Mean = .42	Var = .2724
$\nabla_1^2 z_t$	1 - 4	-.32 -.15 -.30 .46	-.32 -.27 -.53 .10
	5 - 8	-.12 .15 -.49 .37	-.11 .22 -.33 .11
	9 -12	-.12 .14 -.31 .20	-.20 -.13 -.10 -.20
		Mean = .01	Var = .3697
$\nabla_s z_t$	1 - 4	.89 .72 .51 .30	.89 -.41 -.13 -.15
	5 - 8	.14 -.02 -.16 -.23	.13 -.27 -.03 .21
	9 -12	-.25 -.24 -.19 -.11	-.05 -.05 .11 .20
		Mean = 1.73	Var = 1.78
$\nabla_1 \nabla_s z_t$	1 - 4	.36 .12 .02 -.23	.36 -.01 -.02 -.26
	5 - 8	.01 -.08 -.35 -.20	.21 -.16 -.36 -.01
	9 -12	-.22 -.25 -.16 -.16	-.04 -.27 -.28 .00
		Mean = .02	Var = .3427

Model identification:

The first differencing seems to be enough to induce stationarity. Further differencing is not necessary as it increases the variability. Significant autocorrelations of the first differences appear at lags 1 and 4. Those at higher lags may be ignored. The tentatively identified model is

$$(1-B)z_t = \theta_0 + a_t + \theta_1 a_{t-1} + \theta_4 a_{t-4}.$$

Fitting and diagnostic checking:

The fitted model is

$$(1-B)z_t = .41 + a_t + \underset{(.09)}{.56} a_{t-1} + \underset{(.09)}{.51} a_{t-4}.$$

$\hat{\sigma}_a = .45$; Box-Pierce χ^2 (12-3) = 13.79

Corresponding econometric model:

$$\frac{ABKW}{GDPT_{-1}} = \underset{(0.0207)}{-0.0382} - \underset{(0.0027)}{0.0038} \, QS2 - \underset{(0.0029)}{0.0063} \, QS3$$

$$\underset{(0.0047)}{-0.0086} \, QS4 + \underset{(0.1606)}{0.6942} \left(\frac{ABKW}{GDPT_{-1}}\right)_{-1}$$

$$\underset{(0.0007)}{-0.0015} \, RW + \underset{(0.0005)}{0.0012} \, RSUS$$

$$\underset{(0.0356)}{+0.1112} \, \frac{GDPN}{GDPT_{-1}}$$

DW = 1.492   R = 0.9256

Post-sample lead 1 ARIMA forecasts compared with actual values, BNM forecasts and composite forecasts

(Domestic commercial bills)

		Quarter 1	Quarter 2	Quarter 3	Quarter 4
	Actual:	37.25	37.03	38.00	38.86
	Forecast:				
1971	BNM	36.84	38.21	38.37	39.61
	ARIMA	36.91	37.85	36.98	38.98
	COMPOSITE	36.86	38.11	37.96	39.43
	Actual:	39.14	41.20	40.47	40.78
	Forecast:				
1972	BNM	38.86	40.09	41.47	41.86
	ARIMA	39.38	39.00	43.35	39.21
	COMPOSITE	39.01	39.77	42.02	41.08
	Actual:	35.45	30.33	29.59	29.78
	Forecast:				
1973	BNM	40.87	37.56	33.55	33.73
	ARIMA	41.95	33.35	27.59	31.92
	COMPOSITE	41.19	36.32	31.80	33.20
	Actual:	29.96	31.58	33.83	35.65
	Forecast:				
1974	BNM	32.91	33.74	34.92	37.54
	ARIMA	25.60	31.27	33.18	33.48
	COMPOSITE	30.76	33.01	34.41	36.35

Series 5: Open market securities held by banks (ABOM) in billions of Deutsche Marks

year	Quarter			
	1	2	3	4
1957	2.92	3.76	5.76	6.40
1958	7.17	7.95	8.27	7.37
1959	6.58	6.61	6.17	6.10
1960	4.95	5.27	6.03	5.92
1961	5.98	5.88	5.85	5.94
1962	5.57	5.19	5.01	5.66
1963	6.04	5.69	5.28	6.15
1964	7.36	6.15	4.84	4.23
1965	4.36	3.76	3.71	3.68
1966	3.57	3.16	2.59	4.01
1967	6.06	7.00	7.80	9.67
1968	11.37	10.79	10.74	10.44
1969	9.19	8.15	6.47	4.76
1970	2.87	3.07	3.23	5.47
1971	7.20	7.06	5.57	5.97
1972	6.66	6.75	6.82	4.52
1973	3.79	3.38	3.64	3.90
1974	3.62	6.52	6.72	8.29

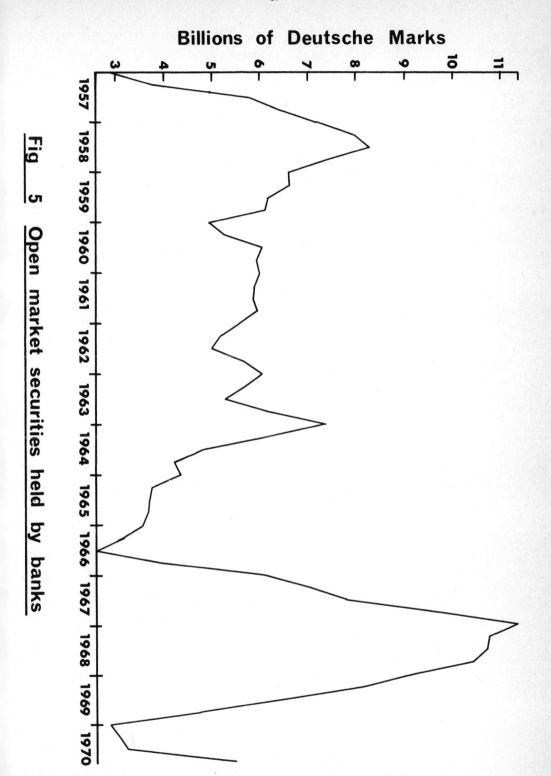

Fig. 5 Open market securities held by banks

Autocorrelations and partial autocorrelations
(Open market securities)

	Lag	Autocorrelations	Partial autocorrelations
z_t	1 - 4	.87 .66 .42 .18	.87 -.49 -.04 -.26
	5 - 8	-.07 -.27 -.40 -.47	-.20 -.01 .03 -.12
	9 -12	-.49 -.46 -.37 -.25	-.03 -.05 .07 -.05
		Mean = 5.96	Var = 4.299
$\nabla_1 z_t$	1 - 4	.50 .19 .10 .09	.50 -.08 .05 .05
	5 - 8	-.15 -.35 -.32 -.28	-.30 -.22 -.04 -.13
	9 -12	-.25 -.32 -.13 .04	-.03 -.21 .06 .03
		Mean = .05	Var = .8989
$\nabla_1^2 z_t$	1 - 4	-.13 -.22 .01 .26	-.13 -.24 -.07 .21
	5 - 8	-.04 -.27 .01 -.05	.02 -.20 -.08 -.23
	9 -12	.11 -.27 -.08 .19	.07 -.22 -.16 .07
		Mean = .03	Var = .8132
$\nabla_s z_t$	1 - 4	.87 .62 .34 .07	.87 -.50 -.19 -.12
	5 - 8	-.16 -.34 -.46 -.51	-.05 -.16 -.11 -.04
	9 -12	-.49 -.41 -.31 -.18	.06 -.13 -.02 -.01
		Mean = -.08	Var = 6.81
$\nabla_1 \nabla_s z_t$	1 - 4	.54 .30 .06 -.15	.54 .01 -.15 -.18
	5 - 8	-.20 -.23 -.37 -.39	-.02 -.07 -.30 -.17
	9 -12	-.25 -.23 -.10 .06	.09 -.19 -.09 .09
		Mean = -.07	Var = 1.48

Model identification:

The series changed its trend four times during the sample period (1957-01 through 1970-04). It started with an upward trend, then changed course and moved downward for some years. It once again moved upward till 1968-01 before taking another downward trend. An upswing seemed to have ensued from the first quarter of 1970.

The original series is highly correlated serially. The autocorrelations are large and positive at lower lags while they are negative and significant at higher lags. The series apparently requires differencing.

The first differencing reduces the variability substantially. The autocorrelation function starts with a significant positive value, declines rapidly then takes negative values and persists significantly at higher lags. Notably, no significant seasonality seems to be present in the data. This is further supported by the fact that the autocorrelation function of the seasonal differences is almost identical with that of the original series itself. Even a second differencing appears to be unnecessary as it brings down the variability by a very small amount from what has been left after the first differencing. Assuming that an autoregressive scheme in conjunction with a drift parameter will take care of the sample autocorrelations, the following model is tentatively suggested.

$$(1 - \phi B)\nabla_1 z_t = \theta_0 + a_t$$

Fitting and diagnostic checking:

The fitted model is

$$(1 - .54B)\nabla_1 z_t = -0.0001 + a_t$$
$$(.13)(.11)$$

$\hat{\sigma}_a = .82$; Box-Pierce χ^2 (12-2) = 12.19

Corresponding econometric model:

$$\frac{ABOM}{BANK}_{-1} = 0.0101 - 0.0030 \, QS2 - 0.0031 \, QS3$$
$$\phantom{\frac{ABOM}{BANK}_{-1} =\ }(0.0027)(0.0008)$$

$$\phantom{\frac{ABOM}{BANK}_{-1} =\ } -0.0004 \, QS4 + 0.7772 \left(\frac{ABOM}{BANK}_{-1}\right)_{-1}$$
$$\phantom{\frac{ABOM}{BANK}_{-1} =\ }(0.0010)(0.0634)$$

$$\phantom{\frac{ABOM}{BANK}_{-1} =\ } +0.0021 \, ROM - 0.0023 \, RFFM$$
$$\phantom{\frac{ABOM}{BANK}_{-1} =\ }(0.0010)(0.0008)$$

$$\phantom{\frac{ABOM}{BANK}_{-1} =\ } -0.2527 \, \frac{(BFLR-BFLR_{-1})}{BANK_{-1}}$$
$$\phantom{\frac{ABOM}{BANK}_{-1} =\ }(0.0387)$$

$$DW = 1.517 \qquad R = 0.9831$$

Post-sample lead 1 ARIMA forecasts compared with actual values,
BNM forecasts and composite forecasts
(Open market securities)

		Quarter			
		1	2	3	4
1971	Actual: Forecast: BNM ARIMA COMPOSITE	7.20 7.16 6.68 7.40	7.06 7.16 8.13 8.04	5.57 7.40 6.98 7.12	5.97 5.89 4.77 5.01
1972	Actual: Forecast: BNM ARIMA COMPOSITE	6.66 10.75 6.19 8.31	6.75 11.41 7.03 8.55	6.82 8.61 6.80 7.22	4.52 9.52 6.86 8.52
1973	Actual: Forecast: BNM ARIMA COMPOSITE	3.79 3.78 3.28 3.02	3.38 .50 3.40 2.17	3.64 -3.58 3.16 .00	3.90 -5.66 3.78 -1.42
1974	Actual: Forecast: BNM ARIMA COMPOSITE	3.62 -4.11 4.04 .62	6.52 -7.38 3.47 -1.71	6.12 -3.24 8.08 3.67	8.29 -.35 5.90 3.10

Series 6: Free liquid reserves of banks (BFLR) in billions of Deutsche Marks

year	Quarter			
	1	2	3	4
1957	9.39	9.25	12.13	14.01
1958	14.97	16.90	17.94	17.85
1959	17.29	18.43	18.73	16.42
1960	11.39	12.62	11.84	13.00
1961	15.59	17.08	18.36	20.48
1962	21.01	19.90	19.11	20.24
1963	19.44	19.50	20.12	22.27
1964	21.93	20.51	18.60	19.85
1965	18.03	17.57	17.63	18.29
1966	16.47	14.84	16.37	20.62
1967	22.96	26.27	29.51	34.77
1968	36.46	36.78	36.91	41.21
1969	35.77	36.72	32.99	27.04
1970	18.85	20.20	22.16	28.09
1971	26.21	33.03	18.01	19.78
1972	35.16	32.89	41.11	41.63
1973	32.85	38.21	44.12	49.45
1974	47.32	52.76	43.68	57.52

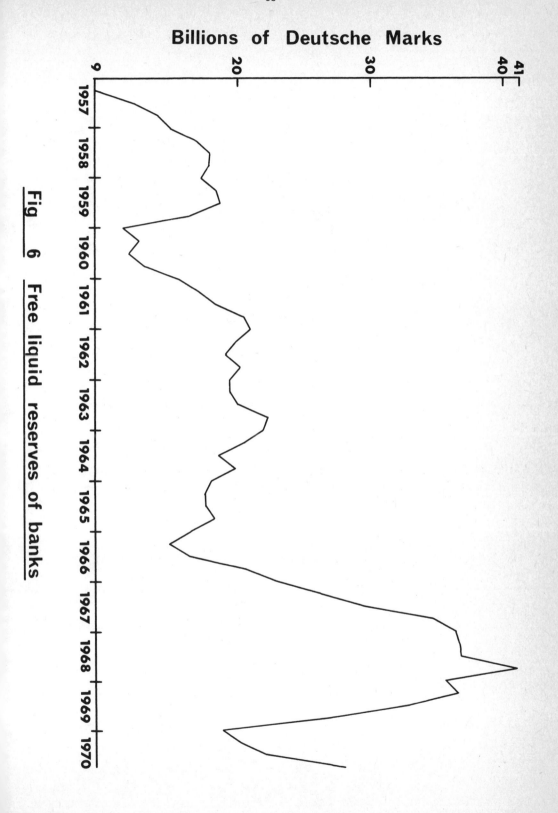

Fig. 6 Free liquid reserves of banks

Autocorrelations and partial autocorrelations
(Free liquid reserves)

	Lag	Autocorrelations	Partial autocorrelations
z_t	1 - 4	.91 .79 .67 .56	.91 -.21 -.10 .04
	5 - 8	.43 .32 .22 .14	-.27 .10 -.06 .04
	9 -12	.07 .04 .03 .03	-.11 .22 .05 -.12
		Mean = 20.94	Var = 56.55
$\nabla_1 z_t$	1 - 4	.33 .20 -.06 .05	.33 .11 -.17 .11
	5 - 8	-.28 -.13 -.25 -.09	-.33 .04 -.14 -.04
	9 -12	-.32 -.21 -.12 .01	-.25 -.18 .07 -.14
		Mean = .34	Var = 6.78
$\nabla_1^2 z_t$	1 - 4	-.38 .11 -.18 .32	-.38 -.04 -.17 .24
	5 - 8	-.41 .16 -.15 .19	-.27 -.09 -.10 .01
	9 -12	-.23 .01 -.05 .12	-.03 -.25 -.10 -.06
		Mean = .11	Var = 8.65
$\nabla_s z_t$	1 - 4	.87 .62 .33 .05	.87 -.54 -.13 -.16
	5 - 8	-.14 -.29 -.42 -.47	.18 -.38 -.11 .07
	9 -12	-.48 -.44 -.35 -.23	-.09 -.09 -.03 .04
		Mean = .86	Var = 44.39
$\nabla_1 \nabla_s z_t$	1 - 4	.44 .15 -.01 -.33	.44 -.05 -.07 -.36
	5 - 8	-.14 -.11 -.16 -.14	.20 -.11 -.27 -.06
	9 -12	-.11 -.19 -.09 -.06	-.11 -.09 -.23 -.01
		Mean = -.09	Var = 11.57

Model identification:

The first differencing reduced the variability to its minimum. It was, therefore, considered that further differencing was unnecessary. For the first differences, the autocorrelations were positive, but declining, at the lower lags, and negative and wavy at the higher lags. Notably, the autocorrelation function did not show any seasonal peaks. As a first step to the development of a model, we fitted a first order autoregressive model

$$(1 - \phi B)\nabla_1 z_t = \theta_0 + \eta_t$$

to the first differences. The autocorrelation function of the residuals, though insignificant, was alternating in sign, starting with a negative value at lag 1. Assuming that a further autoregressing would take care of the residual autocorrelations, we suggested the model

$$(1 - \phi_1 B - \phi_2 B^2)\nabla_1 z_t = \theta_0 + a_t.$$

Fitting and diagnostic checking:

The fitted model is

$$(1 - .32B - .12B^2)\nabla_1 z_t = .19 + a_t$$
$$(.15)(.15)$$

$\hat{\sigma}_a = 2.57$; Box-Pierce χ^2 (12-3) = 8.13.

Corresponding econometric model:

BFLR = SRMAX − PBREF + ABGU − SRSOL + ABOM + ABAK.

Post-sample lead 1 ARIMA forecasts compared with actual values, BNM forecasts and composite forecasts
(Free liquid reserves)

		Quarter 1	Quarter 2	Quarter 3	Quarter 4
1971	Actual:	26.21	33.03	18.01	19.78
	Forecast:				
	BNM	29.67	39.91	35.76	27.04
	ARIMA	30.40	26.50	35.17	14.21
	COMPOSITE	29.87	36.21	35.60	23.50
1972	Actual:	35.16	32.89	41.11	41.63
	Forecast:				
	BNM	33.89	45.47	38.50	44.02
	ARIMA	18.75	40.47	34.18	43.65
	COMPOSITE	29.71	44.10	37.31	43.93
1973	Actual:	32.85	38.21	44.12	49.45
	Forecast:				
	BNM	30.13	22.28	16.41	15.59
	ARIMA	42.96	30.30	39.07	46.83
	COMPOSITE	33.68	24.50	22.67	24.22
1974	Actual:	47.32	52.76	43.68	57.52
	Forecast:				
	BNM	17.77	14.89	24.98	26.73
	ARIMA	52.04	47.46	54.43	41.61
	COMPOSITE	27.24	23.89	33.12	30.85

Series 7: Money (currency + demand deposits) held by banks
(BGM1) in billions of Deutsche Marks

year	Quarter			
	1	2	3	4
1957	32.47	34.24	36.31	38.49
1958	36.90	38.32	39.25	41.51
1959	41.04	43.21	44.56	46.57
1960	45.45	47.08	47.93	49.78
1961	48.93	50.97	53.32	56.21
1962	54.91	57.25	58.69	61.33
1963	59.17	61.01	63.05	65.62
1964	64.00	66.53	68.26	71.08
1965	69.93	72.85	74.18	76.95
1966	74.23	76.81	77.25	78.37
1967	75.44	77.78	79.71	84.04
1968	81.12	83.57	85.68	90.28
1969	86.79	90.53	93.61	97.48
1970	92.83	96.20	99.12	103.89
1971	101.09	107.77	112.33	117.63
1972	114.72	121.65	127.84	134.58
1973	129.50	132.25	129.90	135.84
1974	130.77	137.09	141.37	150.39

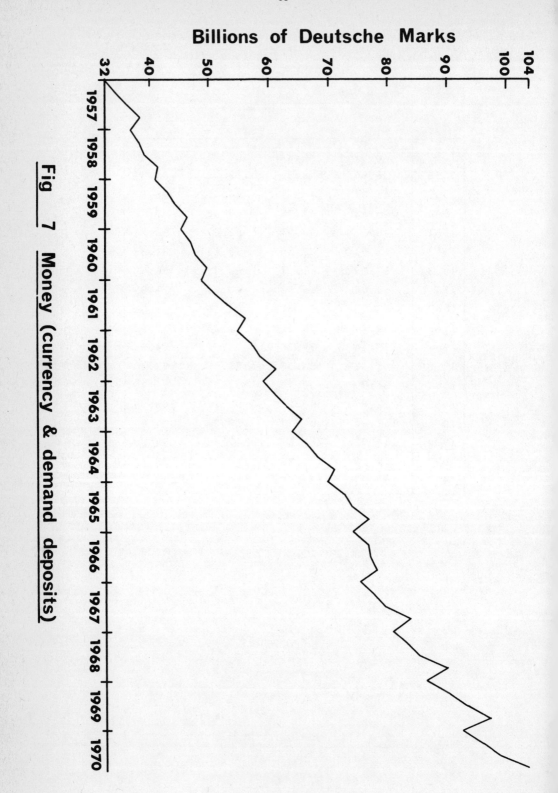

Fig 7 Money (currency & demand deposits)

Autocorrelations and partial autocorrelations
(Money)

	Lag	Autocorrelations	Partial autocorrelations
z_t	1 - 4	.93 .87 .82 .78	.93 .06 .01 .06
	5 - 8	.71 .66 .61 .56	-.19 .02 -.01 .03
	9 -12	.50 .46 .41 .38	-.12 .03 -.01 .01
		Mean = 65.04	Var = 376.5
$\nabla_1 z_t$	1 - 4	-.40 .04 -.46 .80	-.40 -.14 -.60 .63
	5 - 8	-.40 .05 -.39 .69	-.23 -.11 .13 .02
	9 -12	-.34 .04 -.40 .61	.02 -.06 -.05 .04
		Mean = 1.30	Var = 4.53
$\nabla_1^2 z_t$	1 - 4	-.66 .34 -.60 .85	-.66 -.17 -.81 .20
	5 - 8	-.59 .32 -.52 .73	.03 -.12 -.12 -.06
	9 -12	-.50 .29 -.48 .64	.07 .05 -.07 -.05
		Mean = .06	Var = 12.63
$\nabla_s z_t$	1 - 4	.83 .55 .27 .01	.83 -.41 -.14 -.11
	5 - 8	-.15 -.24 -.29 -.28	.05 -.10 -.06 .00
	9 -12	-.26 -.22 -.17 -.12	-.12 .05 -.06 -.01
		Mean = 4.81	Var = 2.17
$\nabla_1 \nabla_s z_t$	1 - 4	.34 .01 -.12 -.32	.34 -.12 -.10 -.28
	5 - 8	-.23 -.12 -.11 -.05	-.04 -.07 -.14 -.11
	9 -12	-.09 -.02 .00 .10	-.18 -.04 -.14 .02
		Mean = .04	Var = .7174

Model identification:

This is a clearly a homogeneous non-stationary series with distinct seasonal pattern. The suggested model is

$$(1-B)(1-B^4)z_t = (1-\theta_1 B)(1-\theta_1 B^4)a_t.$$

Fitting and diagnostic checking:

The fitted model is

$$(1-B)(1-B^4)z_t = .05 + \underset{(.14)}{(1 + .32B)} \underset{(.15)}{(1 - .30B^4)} a_t.$$

$\hat{\sigma}_a = .77$; Box-Pierce $\chi^2 (12-2) = 6.10$

Corresponding econometric model:

BGM1 = NP + PBDSI

Post-sample lead 1 ARIMA forecasts compared with actual values, BNM forecasts and composite forecasts

(Money)

		Quarter			
		1	2	3	4
1971	Actual: Forecast: BNM ARIMA COMPOSITE	101.09 91.49 99.24 97.67	107.77 100.64 105.05 104.21	112.33 99.28 111.56 109.02	117.63 113.16 117.35 116.57
1972	Actual: Forecast: BNM ARIMA COMPOSITE	114.72 111.51 114.36 113.88	121.65 110.97 120.51 118.58	127.84 109.87 126.08 122.71	134.58 110.45 133.54 128.69
1973	Actual: Forecast: BNM ARIMA COMPOSITE	129.50 122.85 131.86 130.06	132.25 135.11 135.30 135.42	129.90 148.05 136.83 139.42	135.84 144.51 133.96 136.40
1974	Actual: Forecast: BNM ARIMA COMPOSITE	130.77 133.58 131.97 132.48	137.09 137.07 134.29 135.05	141.37 127.77 138.02 135.95	150.39 128.22 148.47 144.25

Series 8: Liquidity ratio (BLQ)

year	Quarter 1	2	3	4
1957	.08910	.08506	.10668	.11719
1958	.12149	.13323	.13740	.13304
1959	.12617	.13048	.12804	.10775
1960	.07651	.07777	.07077	.07484
1961	.08638	.09071	.09456	.10238
1962	.10250	.09580	.08917	.09136
1963	.08618	.08432	.08432	.08961
1964	.08663	.07921	.07033	.07226
1965	.06405	.06087	.05956	.05969
1966	.05263	.04632	.04995	.06120
1967	.06717	.07543	.08325	.09426
1968	.09651	.09475	.09281	.09891
1969	.08459	.08387	.07302	.05795
1970	.03960	.04139	.04376	.05319
1971	.0479	.0585	.0310	.0328
1972	.0565	.0508	.0608	.0591
1973	.0445	.0499	.0563	.0611
1974	.0578	.0630	.0517	.0660

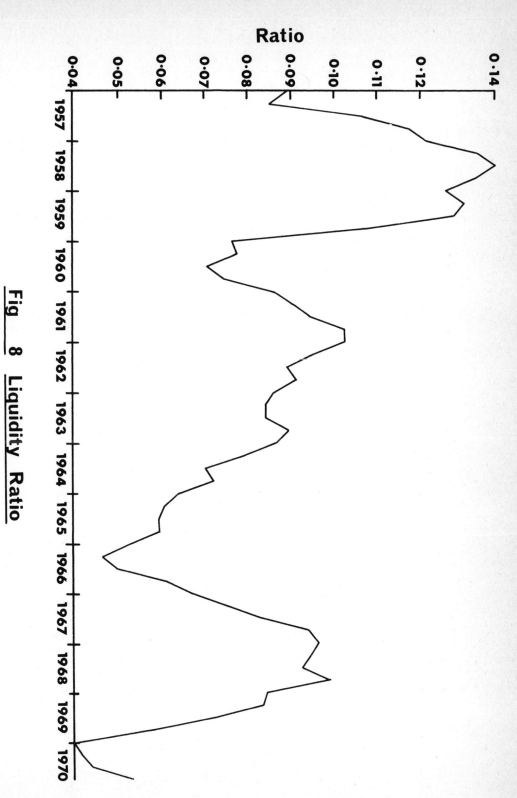

Fig 8 Liquidity Ratio

Autocorrelations and partial autocorrelations
(Liquidity ratio)

	Lag	Autocorrelations	Partial autocorrelations
z_t	1 - 4	.92 .77 .60 .41	.92 -.44 -.14 -.14
	5 - 8	.23 .11 .02 -.04	.00 .16 -.02 -.03
	9 -12	-.06 -.04 .01 .06	.07 .09 .09 -.02
		Mean = .08	Var = .0005
$\nabla_1 z_t$	1 - 4	.40 .17 .07 .03	.40 .01 .00 .00
	5 - 8	-.26 -.23 -.24 -.19	-.32 -.03 -.12 -.05
	9 -12	-.34 -.20 -.04 -.01	-.26 -.06 .04 -.11
		Mean = -.0007	Var = .0001
$\nabla_1^2 z_t$	1 - 4	-.28 -.13 -.01 .21	-.28 -.22 -.13 .16
	5 - 8	-.28 .00 -.02 .14	-.21 -.11 -.15 .03
	9 -12	-.23 -.03 .09 .00	-.17 -.22 -.08 -.16
		Mean = .0002	Var = .0001
$\nabla_s z_t$	1 - 4	.85 .56 .25 -.06	.85 -.60 -.06 -.22
	5 - 8	-.27 -.41 -.50 -.50	.12 -.34 -.02 -.01
	9 -12	-.42 -.30 -.16 -.05	.01 -.09 -.02 -.24
		Mean = -.004	Var = .0006
$\nabla_1 \nabla_s z_t$	1 - 4	.48 .19 .00 -.32	.48 -.06 -.09 -.36
	5 - 8	-.22 -.20 -.28 -.16	.12 -.11 -.21 -.08
	9 -12	-.17 -.07 .05 -.02	-.12 .03 -.09 -.16
		Mean = -.0007	Var = .0001

Model identification:

A first differencing brings down the variability by a substantial amount. No further reduction is achieved by the subsequent differencings. A first order autoregressive scheme will clearly take care of the first few autocorrelations of the first differences. As a first step, therefore, the model

$$(1 - \phi_1 B)\nabla_1 z_t = n_t$$

is fitted. The residual autocorrelations are usually insignificant, though large positive peaks appear at lags 4 and 8. To take care of these autos, the model

$$(1 - \phi_1 B)\nabla_1 z_t = a_t + \theta_4 a_{t-4} + \theta_8 a_{t-8}$$

is tentatively identified.

Fitting and diagnostic checking:

The fitted model is

$$(1 - .49B)\nabla_1 z_t = a_t + .20 a_{t-4} + .08 a_{t-8}.$$
$$(.13) \qquad\qquad (.15) \qquad (.17)$$

$\hat{\sigma}_a = .008$; Box-Pierce $\chi^2 (9) = 6.22$

Corresponding econometric model:

$$BLQ = \frac{BFLR}{PBDSI + PBDTE + PBDSP + PBAK + PBAS + PBIS + PBDIF}$$

Post-sample lead 1 ARIMA forecasts compared with actual values,
BNM forecasts and composite forecasts
(Liquidity ratio)

		Quarter			
		1	2	3	4
1971	Actual:	.048	.059	.031	.033
	Forecast:				
	BNM	.055	.053	.061	.046
	ARIMA	.058	.045	.064	.018
	COMPOSITE	.056	.050	.062	.033
1972	Actual:	.057	.051	.061	.059
	Forecast:				
	BNM	.055	.070	.057	.063
	ARIMA	.032	.071	.042	.069
	COMPOSITE	.045	.070	.050	.066
1973	Actual:	.045	.050	.056	.061
	Forecast:				
	BNM	.042	.030	.022	.021
	ARIMA	.062	.035	.054	.059
	COMPOSITE	.051	.032	.036	.038
1974	Actual:	.059	.063	.052	.066
	Forecast:				
	BNM	.023	.019	.031	.032
	ARIMA	.062	.058	.068	.046
	COMPOSITE	.040	.036	.047	.038

Series 9: Loans to the banks held by the Bundesbank (PBREF) in billions of Deutsche Marks

year	Quarter 1	2	3	4
1957	1.82	2.27	1.57	1.18
1958	1.21	1.25	0.88	0.74
1959	0.73	0.73	0.79	1.15
1960	1.64	1.45	1.84	1.74
1961	1.54	1.01	1.33	1.33
1962	1.16	1.39	1.62	1.49
1963	1.89	2.75	1.99	1.69
1964	2.06	2.84	3.65	3.40
1965	4.10	4.39	5.30	5.24
1966	6.58	7.57	6.80	6.04
1967	5.57	6.27	5.39	4.52
1968	5.07	5.32	5.99	5.95
1969	9.08	8.01	8.45	13.66
1970	19.16	19.67	19.25	17.75
1971	19.39	14.79	20.69	19.09
1972	16.92	18.15	17.82	18.48
1973	14.73	10.28	11.45	10.22
1974	10.40	10.96	15.85	14.48

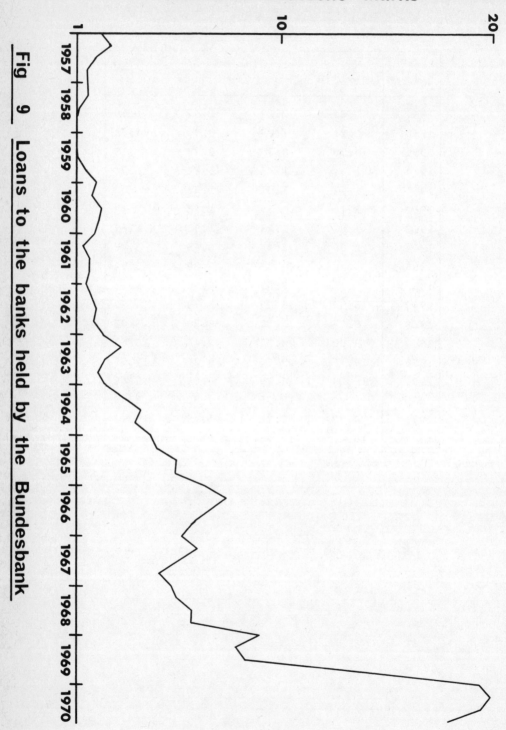

Fig 9 Loans to the banks held by the Bundesbank

Autocorrelations and partial autocorrelations
(Loans to banks held by Bundesbank)

	Lags	Autocorrelations	Partial autocorrelations
z_t	1 - 4	.90 .75 .61 .46	.90 -.25 -.07 -.07
	5 - 8	.37 .32 .29 .22	.15 .13 -.11 -.14
	9 -12	.20 .19 .19 .19	.22 .04 .04 -.13
		Mean = 4.59	Var = 22.92
$\nabla_1 z_t$	1 - 4	.34 -.09 -.06 .12	.34 -.22 .06 .12
	5 - 8	-.01 -.03 .01 -.09	-.13 .06 .00 -.16
	9 -12	-.18 -.09 .04 -.02	-.07 -.02 .03 -.05
		Mean = .29	Var = 1.46
$\nabla_1^2 z_t$	1 - 4	-.17 -.33 -.03 .23	-.17 -.37 -.20 .06
	5 - 8	-.16 -.08 .18 -.06	-.19 -.08 .09 -.12
	9 -12	-.12 -.05 .16 .03	-.06 -.15 -.04 .04
		Mean = -.04	Var = 1.91
$\nabla_s z_t$	1 - 4	.86 .62 .40 .22	.86 -.44 .02 -.02
	5 - 8	.12 .03 -.08 -.16	.13 -.30 -.03 -.01
	9 -12	-.19 -.19 -.17 -.13	.16 -.23 .10 .05
		Mean = 1.32	Var = 8.18
$\nabla_1 \nabla_s z_t$	1 - 4	.18 -.07 -.15 -.27	.18 -.11 -.12 -.24
	5 - 8	.13 .04 -.11 -.16	.23 -.10 -.15 -.17
	9 -12	-.09 -.03 -.10 -.03	.06 -.14 -.24 -.06
		Mean = .09	Var = 2.13

Model identification:

The first differencing seems to be enough to induce stationarity. Also at this stage the variability is a minimum. Tentatively identified model is

$$(1-B)z_t = \theta_0 + a_t + \theta_1 a_{t-1}.$$

Fitting and diagnostic checking:

The fitted model is

$$(1-B)z_t = \underset{(.22)}{.28} + a_t + \underset{(.13)}{.43 a_{t-1}}$$

$\hat{\sigma}_a = 1.13$; Box-Pierce χ^2 (12-2) = 4.19

Corresponding econometric model:

$$\frac{PBREF}{BANK_{-1}} = \underset{(0.0021)}{-0.0044} - \underset{(0.0013)}{0.0006 \ QS2} - \underset{(0.0013)}{0.0019 \ QS3}$$

$$\underset{(0.0015)}{-0.0046 \ QS4} + \underset{(0.1228)}{0.4877} \left(\frac{PBREF}{BANK_{-1}}\right)_{-1}$$

$$\underset{(0.0015)}{-0.0013 \ RDISK} + \underset{(0.0010)}{0.0028 \ RFFM}$$

$$\underset{(0.0004)}{+0.0014 \ RSUS.}$$

$$DW = 1.738 \qquad R = 0.9684$$

Post-sample lead 1 ARIMA forecasts compared with actual values, BNM forecasts and composite forecasts

(Loans to banks held by Bundesbank)

		Quarter 1	Quarter 2	Quarter 3	Quarter 4
	Actual:	19.39	14.79	20.69	19.09
	Forecast:				
1971	BNM	15.91	16.48	13.15	17.95
	ARIMA	18.03	20.25	12.75	24.36
	COMPOSITE	15.99	16.54	13.27	17.97
	Actual:	16.92	18.15	17.82	18.48
	Forecast:				
1972	BNM	15.15	11.60	13.96	13.33
	ARIMA	17.13	17.11	18.87	17.65
	COMPOSITE	15.23	11.57	13.97	13.35
	Actual:	14.73	10.28	11.45	10.22
	Forecast:				
1973	BNM	18.46	18.18	17.85	19.88
	ARIMA	19.12	13.14	9.34	12.63
	COMPOSITE	18.61	18.45	18.20	20.21
	Actual:	10.40	10.96	15.85	14.48
	Forecast:				
1974	BNM	20.79	19.69	17.69	20.70
	ARIMA	9.48	11.08	11.19	18.12
	COMPOSITE	21.22	20.05	17.99	20.94

Series 10: 90-day-money-rate Frankfurt (RFFM)

year	Quarter			
	1	2	3	4
1957	4.94	5.19	3.19	3.56
1958	3.84	3.72	3.19	2.54
1959	2.93	2.82	2.84	4.37
1960	4.49	4.78	5.54	5.53
1961	4.17	3.23	3.13	3.86
1962	2.99	3.11	3.27	4.40
1963	3.41	3.70	3.88	5.04
1964	3.41	3.66	3.95	5.37
1965	4.06	4.66	5.22	6.53
1966	5.43	6.46	6.90	7.73
1967	5.43	4.05	3.50	4.09
1968	3.43	3.68	3.56	4.49
1969	4.00	4.76	6.39	7.98
1970	9.45	9.56	9.31	8.85
1971	7.49	6.41	7.60	7.06
1972	4.96	4.71	4.92	7.85
1973	8.21	12.22	14.37	13.77
1974	11.32	9.54	9.61	9.14

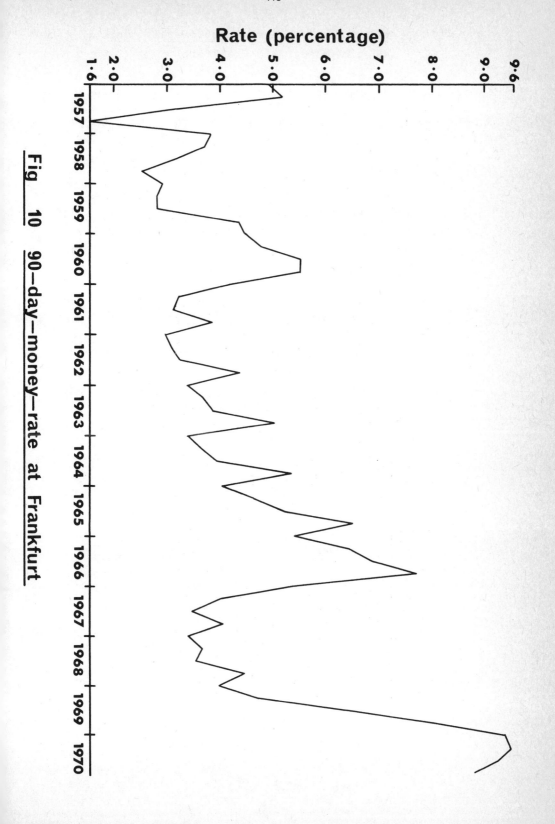

Fig 10 90-day-money-rate at Frankfurt

Autocorrelations and partial autocorrelations
(90-day-money rate-Frankfurt)

	Lags	Autocorrelations	Partial autocorrelations
z_t	1 - 4	.80 .59 .40 .25	.80 -.15 -.09 .02
	5 - 8	.03 -.08 -.12 -.10	-.36 .17 .05 .02
	9 -12	-.16 -.12 -.05 .09	-.20 .21 .01 .22

Mean = 4.67   Var = 3.22

	Lags	Autocorrelations	Partial autocorrelations
$\nabla_1 z_t$	1 - 4	.00 -.06 -.18 .37	.00 -.06 -.18 .38
	5 - 8	-.25 -.11 -.15 .23	-.35 -.06 -.03 -.01
	9 -12	-.29 -.09 -.22 .20	-.22 -.07 -.25 .00

Mean = .07   Var = .9651

	Lags	Autocorrelations	Partial autocorrelations
$\nabla_1^2 z_t$	1 - 4	-.46 .03 -.34 .59	-.46 -.24 -.58 .20
	5 - 8	-.37 .08 -.22 .47	-.14 -.15 -.15 .06
	9 -12	-.37 .17 -.28 .34	-.13 .03 -.22 -.25

Mean = -.01   Var = 1.96

	Lags	Autocorrelations	Partial autocorrelations
$\nabla_s z_t$	1 - 4	.83 .52 .20 -.03	.83 -.54 -.03 .01
	5 - 8	-.19 -.29 -.33 -.36	-.17 -.05 -.06 -.22
	9 -12	-.39 -.34 -.21 -.04	-.12 .26 -.08 .06

Mean = .43   Var = 3.10

	Lags	Autocorrelations	Partial autocorrelations
$\nabla_1 \nabla_s z_t$	1 - 4	.40 .03 -.23 -.25	.40 -.16 -.22 -.08
	5 - 8	-.19 -.14 .28 -.01	-.08 -.12 .06 -.15
	9 -12	-.24 -.20 -.16 .10	-.37 -.03 -.19 .03

Mean = .04   Var = 1.03

Model identification:

The series requires differencing. The first difference of the seasonal differences seems to be stationary though the variability of this series is slightly more than that of the first differences. A tentatively selected model is

$$(1-B)(1-B^4)z_t = (1 - \theta_1 B)(1 - \theta_4 B^4)a_t.$$

Fitting and diagnostic checking:

The fitted model is

$$(1-B)(1-B^4)z_t = \underset{(.14)}{(1 + .36B)} \underset{(.16)}{(1 - .21B^4)} a_t$$

$\hat{\sigma}_a = .93$; Box-Pierce χ^2 (12-2) = 10.69

Alternatively, for the seasonal-mean-adjusted series the fitted model is

$$(1-B)z_t - \hat{\alpha}_t = (1 + \underset{(.08)}{.22B} - \underset{(.14)}{.44B^3} - \underset{(.17)}{.24B^6} - \underset{(.16)}{.32B^9})a_t$$

$\hat{\sigma}_a = .68$; Box-Pierce χ^2 (12-4) = 6.67

$\hat{\alpha}_t$ = observed seasonal mean.

The alternative model, with a smaller Box-Pierce χ^2 values, was accepted for further use.

Corresponding econometric model:

$$\begin{aligned}
\text{RFFM} = &-0.3487 + 0.0180\ \text{QS2} + 0.2246\ \text{QS3} \\
&(0.2539)\ \ (0.2086)\quad\quad (0.2072) \\
&+1.0363\ \text{QS4} + 0.7326\ \text{RFFM}_{-1} \\
&(0.2002)\quad\quad (0.1043) \\
&+0.8243\ \text{RDISK} - 41.9947\ (\text{BLQ}_{-1} - \text{BLQ}_{-2}) \\
&(0.1556)\quad\quad\quad (11.6940)
\end{aligned}$$

$$\text{DW} = 2.340 \qquad R = 0.9817$$

Post-sample lead 1 ARIMA forecasts compared with actual values, BNM forecasts and composite forecasts
(90-day-money-rate Frankfurt)

		Quarter 1	Quarter 2	Quarter 3	Quarter 4
1971	Actual:	7.49	6.41	7.60	7.06
	Forecast:				
	BNM	7.45	6.80	5.94	8.38
	ARIMA	8.19	7.42	6.12	9.01
	COMPOSITE	7.54	6.80	5.94	8.37
1972	Actual:	4.96	4.71	4.92	7.85
	Forecast:				
	BNM	5.19	3.06	4.34	5.40
	ARIMA	6.42	4.08	5.79	6.40
	COMPOSITE	5.20	3.07	4.37	5.38
1973	Actual:	8.21	12.22	14.37	13.77
	Forecast:				
	BNM	6.76	8.23	9.97	11.51
	ARIMA	6.88	9.65	12.73	14.30
	COMPOSITE	6.78	8.23	10.03	11.59
1974	Actual:	11.32	9.54	9.61	9.14
	Forecast:				
	BNM	10.35	9.79	8.98	9.85
	ARIMA	12.71	10.52	8.97	10.82
	COMPOSITE	10.38	9.86	8.99	9.85

Series 11: Interest rates on current account loans (RKONT)

year	Quarter 1	2	3	4
1957	10.50	10.50	10.33	10.00
1958	9.50	9.42	9.00	9.00
1959	8.75	8.75	8.83	10.00
1960	10.00	10.33	11.00	10.33
1961	9.50	9.17	9.00	9.00
1962	9.00	9.00	9.00	9.00
1963	9.00	9.00	9.00	9.00
1964	9.00	9.00	9.00	9.00
1965	9.50	9.50	9.83	10.00
1966	10.00	10.67	11.00	11.00
1967	10.17	7.72	7.64	7.62
1968	7.60	7.59	7.55	7.52
1969	7.51	8.01	8.94	9.60
1970	10.15	11.58	11.40	11.35
1971	10.66	10.12	9.87	9.68
1972	9.05	8.61	8.40	8.86
1973	10.00	11.32	13.16	14.02
1974	13.92	13.77	13.55	13.15

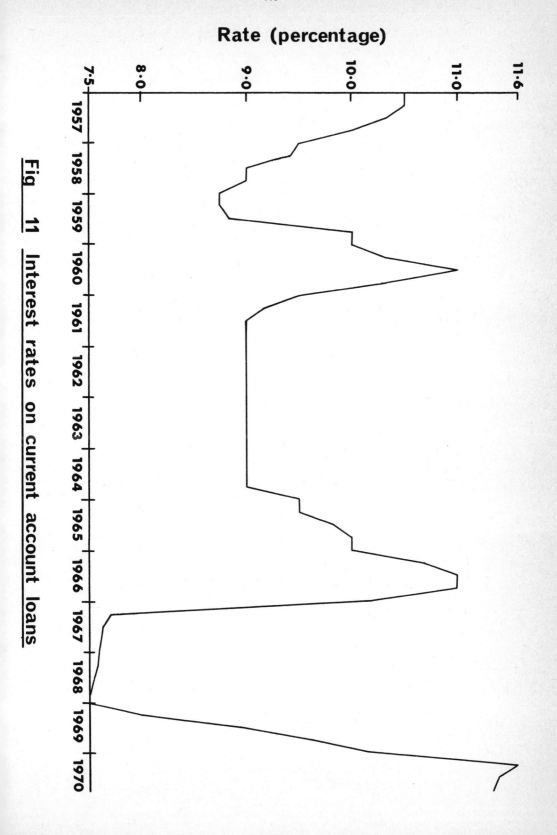

Fig 11 Interest rates on current account loans

Autocorrelations and partial autocorrelations
(Interest rates on current account loans)

	Lags	Autocorrelations	Partial autocorrelations
z_t	1 - 4	.83 .57 .28 .03	.83 -.39 -.23 -.04
	5 - 8	-.17 -.32 -.41 -.46	-.08 -.15 -.08 -.12
	9 -12	-.47 -.41 -.31 -.21	-.11 .04 -.05 -.13
		Mean = 9.36	Var = 1.11
$\nabla_1 z_t$	1 - 4	.36 .13 .05 -.12	.36 .01 .00 -.16
	5 - 8	-.10 -.08 -.11 -.15	-.01 -.03 -.07 -.12
	9 -12	-.27 -.16 -.10 -.17	-.22 -.01 -.04 -.18
		Mean = .02	Var = .28
$\nabla_1^2 z_t$	1 - 4	-.33 -.10 .06 -.15	-.33 -.24 -.06 -.20
	5 - 8	.00 .04 .00 .06	-.15 -.10 -.05 .02
	9 -12	-.17 .03 .10 -.23	-.20 -.13 .00 -.26
		Mean = .0009	Var = .37
$\nabla_s z_t$	1 - 4	.83 .54 .21 -.07	.83 -.46 -.23 -.05
	5 - 8	-.19 -.27 -.32 -.35	.24 -.34 -.20 .00
	9 -12	-.39 -.36 -.27 -.15	-.07 .02 -.06 .04
		Mean = .06	Var = 1.978
$\nabla_1 \nabla_s z_t$	1 - 4	.33 .04 -.10 -.47	.33 -.07 -.11 -.46
	5 - 8	-.11 -.01 .00 .04	.25 -.08 -.04 -.25
	9 -12	-.22 -.14 -.06 -.03	-.16 -.02 -.04 -.11
		Mean = .05	Var = .62

Model identification:

The autocorrelations suggest the following model:

$$(1-B)z_t = \theta_0 + a_t + \theta_1 a_{t-1}.$$

Fitting and diagnostic checking:

$$(1-B)z_t = \underset{(.09)}{.02} + a_t + \underset{(.13)}{.34} a_{t-1}.$$

$\hat{\sigma}_a = .51$; Box-Pierce $\chi^2 (12-2) = 5.75$

Corresponding econometric model:

$$\text{RKONT} = \underset{(7.7734)}{-11.6619} - \underset{(0.2044)}{0.4220}\ \text{QS2} - \underset{(0.1993)}{0.2743}\ \text{QS3}$$

$$\underset{(0.2013)}{-0.2598}\ \text{QS4} + \underset{(0.1257)}{0.5182}\ \text{RKONT}_{-1}$$

$$\underset{(8.5518)}{+8.3407}\ \frac{\text{ABKS}}{\text{BANK}_{-1}} + \underset{(0.2954)}{0.7194}\ \text{ROBLD}$$

$$\underset{(0.1579)}{+0.2775}\ \text{RLGB} + \underset{(278.7124)}{740.4585}\ \frac{1}{\text{BANK}_{-1}}$$

$$\underset{(9.5397)}{+37.4204}\ \frac{\text{BFLR}_{-1} - \text{BFLR}_{-2}}{\text{BANK}_{-1}}$$

DW = 1.950   R = 0.9492

Post-sample lead 1 ARIMA forecasts compared with actual values, BNM forecasts and composite forecasts
(Interest rates on current account loans)

		Quarter			
		1	2	3	4
1971	Actual:	10.66	10.12	9.87	9.68
	Forecast:				
	BNM	10.	10.32	9.49	11.12
	ARIMA	11.37	10.44	10.03	9.83
	COMPOSITE	11.08	10.51	9.69	11.24
1972	Actual:	9.05	8.61	8.40	8.86
	Forecast:				
	BNM	9.66	7.80	8.96	8.41
	ARIMA	9.64	8.86	8.54	8.37
	COMPOSITE	9.83	8.00	9.09	8.56
1973	Actual:	10.00	11.32	13.16	14.02
	Forecast:				
	BNM	9.65	10.69	11.76	13.02
	ARIMA	9.04	10.34	11.67	13.68
	COMPOSITE	9.79	10.86	11.97	13.29
1974	Actual:	13.92	13.77	13.55	13.15
	Forecast:				
	BNM	14.11	14.41	14.38	15.13
	ARIMA	14.15	13.86	13.76	13.50
	COMPOSITE	14.36	14.63	14.60	15.31

Series 12: Yield on officially quoted bonds in Germany
(ROBLD)

year	Quarter			
	1	2	3	4
1957	5.90	5.90	6.00	6.10
1958	6.00	6.00	5.90	5.80
1959	5.70	5.80	5.60	5.60
1960	6.20	6.30	6.50	6.30
1961	6.10	5.70	5.90	6.00
1962	5.90	5.90	6.10	6.20
1963	6.10	6.10	6.10	6.10
1964	6.00	6.20	6.30	6.30
1965	6.40	6.70	7.00	7.30
1966	7.30	7.70	8.10	7.80
1967	7.30	6.90	6.90	7.00
1968	7.00	6.80	6.60	6.50
1969	6.50	6.80	7.10	7.30
1970	7.70	8.30	8.50	8.50
1971	7.93	8.13	8.47	8.20
1972	7.80	8.17	8.33	8.57
1973	8.64	9.70	9.99	9.68
1974	10.28	10.80	10.86	10.32

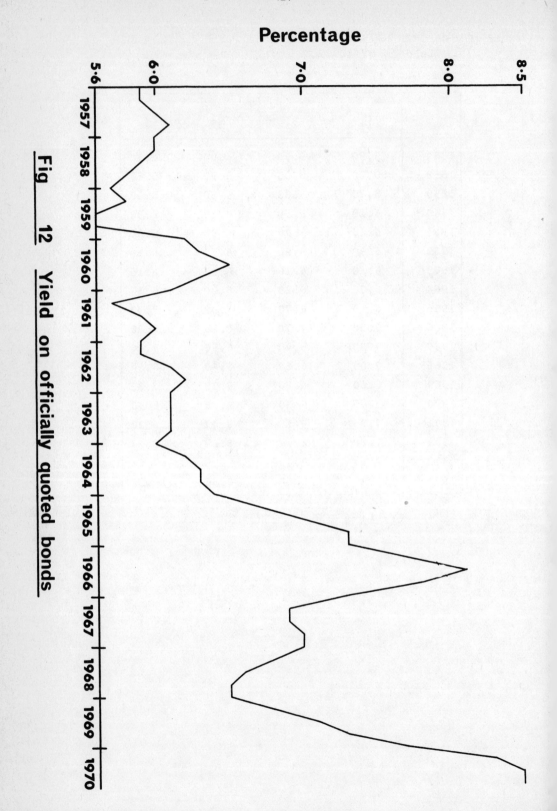

Fig 12 Yield on officially quoted bonds

Autocorrelations and Partial Autocorrelations
(Yield on officially quoted bonds in Germany)

	Lags	Autocorrelations	Partial autocorrelations
z_t	1 – 4	.88 .73 .58 .47	.88 –.26 –.02 .09
	5 – 8	.38 .31 .26 .24	–.04 .01 .06 .06
	9 –12	.24 .24 .23 .22	.03 .02 –.02 .00
		Mean = 6.54	Var = .56
$\nabla_1 z_t$	1 – 4	.43 .05 –.04 .00	.43 –.17 .01 .04
	5 – 8	–.09 –.11 –.14 –.22	–.15 .00 –.11 –.18
	9 –12	–.11 –.11 –.10 –.20	.08 –.18 –.20 –.21
		Mean = .04	Var = .05
$\nabla_1^2 z_t$	1 – 4	–.16 –.25 –.13 .13	–.15 –.28 –.24 –.04
	5 – 8	–.07 .00 .04 –.16	–.18 –.07 –.02 –.25
	9 –12	.09 –.02 .12 –.13	.01 –.15 .04 –.10
		Mean = .00	Var = .0585
$\nabla_s z_t$	1 – 4	.83 .52 .18 –.08	.83 –.57 –.09 .01
	5 – 8	–.21 –.28 –.31 –.32	.05 –.20 –.13 –.03
	9 –12	–.31 –.32 –.32 –.27	–.07 –.26 –.04 .11
		Mean = .18	Var = .35
$\nabla_1 \nabla_s z_t$	1 – 4	.48 .04 –.22 –.37	.48 –.25 –.17 –.23
	5 – 8	–.21 –.02 .03 –.04	.09 –.01 –.11 –.16
	9 –12	.14 –.07 –.15 –.16	.12 –.17 –.15 –.17
		Mean = .02	Var = .0993

Model identification:

The suggested model is a Noisy Random walk model with a drift.

$$(1-B)z_t = \theta_0 + a_t + \theta_1 a_{t-1}.$$

Fitting and diagnostic checking:

The fitted model is

$$(1-B)z_t = \underset{(.04)}{.05} + a_t + \underset{(.12)}{.44} a_{t-1}.$$

$\hat{\sigma} = .21$; Box-Pierce χ^2 (12-2) = 5.80.

Corresponding econometric model:

$$\text{ROBLD} = \underset{(0.5174)}{2.2608} + \underset{(0.0933)}{0.5326} \text{ROBLD}_{-1} + \underset{(0.0478)}{0.2885} \text{RDISK}$$

$$+ \underset{(2.7728)}{0.6755} \frac{(P-P_{-1})}{P_{-1}} - 5.6058 \frac{\text{GB}}{\text{GDPT}}$$

$$- \underset{(2.1607)}{4.7530} \frac{\text{GB}_{-1}}{\text{GDPT}}$$

$$\text{DW} = 1.278 \qquad R = 0.9792$$

Post-sample lead 1 ARIMA forecasts compared with actual values, BNM forecasts and composite forecasts
(Yield on officially quoted bonds)

		Quarter 1	Quarter 2	Quarter 3	Quarter 4
1971	Actual:	7.93	8.13	8.47	8.20
	Forecast:				
	BNM	8.38	7.78	7.91	8.00
	ARIMA	8.55	7.70	8.37	8.56
	COMPOSITE	8.42	7.77	7.99	8.10
1972	Actual:	7.80	8.17	8.33	8.57
	Forecast:				
	BNM	7.67	7.32	7.51	7.89
	ARIMA	8.09	7.72	8.42	8.34
	COMPOSITE	7.74	7.40	7.67	7.97
1973	Actual:	8.64	9.70	9.99	9.68
	Forecast:				
	BNM	7.99	8.14	9.09	9.38
	ARIMA	8.72	8.65	10.21	9.94
	COMPOSITE	8.12	8.23	9.29	9.48
1974	Actual:	10.28	10.80	10.86	10.32
	Forecast:				
	BNM	9.33	9.67	9.97	9.80
	ARIMA	9.61	10.62	10.93	10.88
	COMPOSITE	9.38	9.84	10.14	9.99

Series 13: Yield on officially quoted shares in Germany
(RAKT)

year	Quarter 1	2	3	4
1957	4.33	4.71	4.70	4.66
1958	4.51	4.41	3.89	3.35
1959	3.23	2.94	2.29	2.31
1960	2.21	2.07	1.79	1.92
1961	2.06	2.11	2.54	2.47
1962	2.61	3.16	3.69	3.56
1963	3.65	3.34	3.12	3.20
1964	2.92	2.96	2.93	3.09
1965	3.19	3.51	3.68	3.93
1966	3.82	4.19	4.62	4.76
1967	4.44	4.45	4.01	3.59
1968	3.33	3.08	2.94	2.98
1969	2.93	3.00	3.06	2.82
1970	3.15	3.69	4.02	4.26
1971	3.86	3.94	3.98	4.19
1972	3.46	2.97	2.87	3.05
1973	2.86	3.16	3.46	3.63
1974	3.77	4.04	4.58	4.51

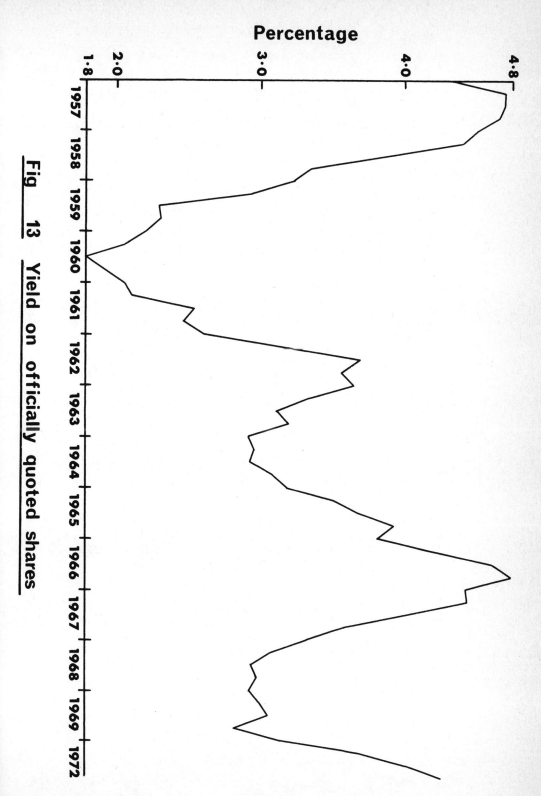

Fig 13 Yield on officially quoted shares

Autocorrelations and partial autocorrelations
(Yield on officially quoted shares in Germany)

	Lags	Autocorrelations	Partial autocorrelations
z_t	1 - 4	.91 .77 .60 .41	.91 -.40 -.15 -.17
	5 - 8	.22 .04 -.12 -.24	-.11 -.11 -.03 .04
	9 -12	-.32 -.36 -.35 -.31	-.02 .05 .08 -.09
		Mean = 3.36	Var = .63
$\nabla_1 z_t$	1 - 4	.43 .29 .27 .13	.43 .12 .13 -.07
	5 - 8	-.09 -.06 -.20 -.30	-.22 .00 -.17 -.14
	9 -12	-.30 -.29 -.24 -.26	-.10 -.09 .01 -.14
		Mean = -.0013	Var = .0782
$\nabla_1^2 z_t$	1 - 4	-.35 -.13 .14 .09	-.35 -.29 -.03 .13
	5 - 8	-.20 .15 -.06 -.08	-.10 .08 -.06 -.10
	9 -12	.03 -.08 .06 -.12	-.06 -.19 .01 -.17
		Mean = -.0026	Var = .0855
$\nabla_s z_t$	1 - 4	.86 .68 .46 .22	.86 -.28 -.20 -.23
	5 - 8	.03 -.15 -.31 -.41	.07 -.18 -.17 -.03
	9 -12	-.46 -.45 -.38 -.28	.05 -.02 .05 .00
		Mean = -.0631	Var = .6471
$\nabla_1 \nabla_s z_t$	1 - 4	.39 .22 .23 -.18	.38 .09 .14 -.39
	5 - 8	-.13 -.04 -.22 -.24	.02 .06 -.12 -.24
	9 -12	-.16 -.26 -.21 -.26	-.03 -.07 -.09 -.36
		Mean = .0247	Var = .1323

Model identification:

The second differencing seems to have induced stationarity with a significant autocorrelation at lag 1 only. The suggested model is

$$(1-B)^2 z_t = a_t + \theta_1 a_{t-1}.$$

Fitting and diagnostic checking:

The fitted model is

$$(1-B)^2 z_t = a_t - \underset{(.12)}{.47} a_{t-1}.$$

$\hat{\sigma}_a = .27$; Box-Pierce $\chi^2 (12-1) = 6.28$

Corresponding econometric model:

$$RAKT = \underset{(0.2757)}{-0.0953} + \underset{(0.0536)}{0.7647} RAKT_{-1} + \underset{(0.0473)}{0.2251} ROBLD$$

$$\underset{(1.6256)}{-7.4673} \; \frac{(YPPN + CCAP - IFNP)}{GDPT_{-1}}$$

$$DW = 1.746 \qquad R = 0.9622$$

Post-sample lead 1 ARIMA forecasts compared with actual values, BNM forecasts and composite forecasts
(Yield on officially quoted shares)

		Quarter			
		1	2	3	4
1971	Actual:	3.86	3.94	3.98	4.19
	Forecast:				
	BNM	4.52	4.31	4.40	4.35
	ARIMA	4.50	3.76	3.94	4.00
	COMPOSITE	4.52	4.23	4.33	4.29
1972	Actual:	3.46	2.97	2.87	3.05
	Forecast:				
	BNM	4.30	3.87	3.54	3.45
	ARIMA	4.31	3.13	2.56	2.62
	COMPOSITE	4.30	3.76	3.40	3.33
1973	Actual:	2.86	3.16	3.46	3.63
	Forecast:				
	BNM	3.30	3.30	3.76	4.00
	ARIMA	3.03	2.75	3.27	3.67
	COMPOSITE	3.26	3.22	3.68	3.96
1974	Actual:	3.77	4.04	4.58	4.51
	Forecast:				
	BNM	4.08	4.39	4.68	4.99
	ARIMA	3.82	3.93	4.26	4.97
	COMPOSITE	4.04	4.32	4.62	4.99

Series 14: Demand deposits (PBDSI) in billions of Deutsche Marks

year	Quarter			
	1	2	3	4
1957	17.34	18.26	19.94	21.63
1958	19.84	20.92	21.50	23.22
1959	22.92	24.48	25.34	27.02
1960	25.95	26.97	27.07	28.69
1961	27.74	29.05	30.60	33.08
1962	31.81	33.41	34.41	36.72
1963	34.59	35.61	37.14	39.45
1964	38.11	39.48	40.59	43.05
1965	41.65	43.46	44.35	46.93
1966	44.53	46.14	45.90	47.33
1967	45.35	46.92	48.48	52.72
1968	50.49	51.95	53.63	57.63
1969	54.53	57.32	59.59	62.81
1970	58.93	61.15	63.07	67.51
1971	65.40	70.37	73.57	78.14
1972	75.42	80.20	84.56	90.34
1973	85.97	86.86	83.64	88.95
1974	85.47	89.35	91.37	99.63

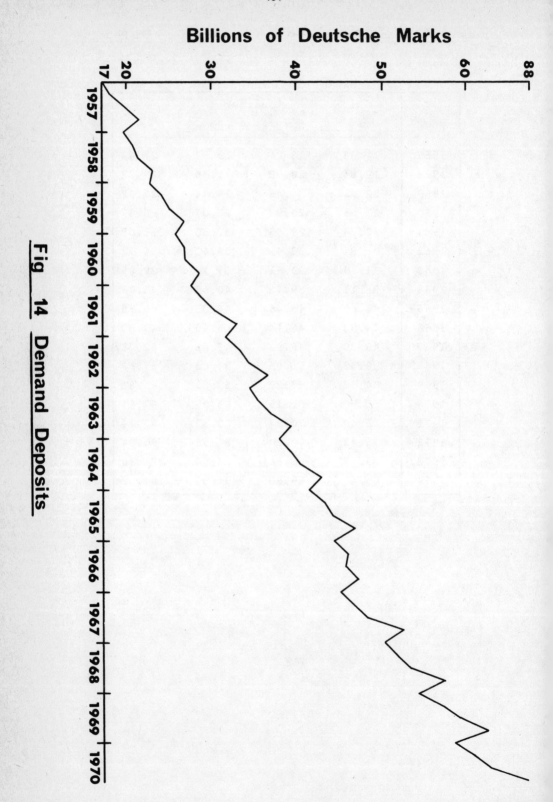

Fig 14 Demand Deposits

Autocorrelations and partial autocorrelations
(Demand deposits)

	Lags	Autocorrelations	Partial autocorrelations
z_t	1 - 4	.93 .87 .82 .78	.93 .08 .01 .08
	5 - 8	.71 .65 .59 .55	-.23 .03 -.01 .05
	9 -12	.49 .44 .40 .36	-.14 .04 .00 .01
		Mean = 39.08	Var = 180.00
$\nabla_1 z_t$	1 - 4	-.40 .06 -.46 .78	-.40 -.12 -.59 .60
	5 - 8	-.41 .08 -.39 .69	-.25 -.09 .12 .08
	9 -12	-.35 .08 -.36 .61	.06 -.03 -.02 .09
		Mean = .9122	Var = 3.225
$\nabla_1^2 z_t$	1 - 4	-.66 .36 -.60 .83	-.66 -.15 -.78 .26
	5 - 8	-.60 .35 -.52 .72	-.00 -.14 -.12 -.05
	9 -12	-.52 .32 -.49 .64	.09 .06 -.11 -.07
		Mean = .0652	Var = 8.977
$\nabla_s z_t$	1 - 4	.79 .51 .22 -.04	.79 -.33 -.15 -.16
	5 - 8	-.15 -.16 -.13 -.08	.18 .02 -.06 -.04
	9 -12	-.06 -.05 -.06 -.04	-.05 .02 -.05 .10
		Mean = 3.33	Var = 1.634
$\nabla_1 \nabla_s z_t$	1 - 4	.27 -.05 -.09 -.38	.27 -.13 -.05 -.38
	5 - 8	-.30 -.07 .00 .00	-.13 -.05 -.06 -.17
	9 -12	.02 .03 -.09 .06	-.16 -.07 -.22 .01
		Mean = .0431	Var = .6330

Model identification:

This is a constituent part of the Money series. It is, therefore, no surprise that this series looks and behaves as the Money series. The identified model is

$$(1-B)(1-B^4)z_t = \theta_0 + (1 - \theta_1 B)(1 - \theta_4 B^4)a_t.$$

Fitting and diagnostic checking:

The fitted model is

$$(1-B)(1-B^4)z_t = .04 + (1 + .27B)(1 - .39B^4)a_t.$$
$$\quad\quad\quad\quad\quad\quad\quad (.14) \quad\quad\quad (.14)$$

$\hat{\sigma}_a = .72$; Box-Pierce χ^2 (12-2) = 6.41

Corresponding econometric model:

$$\frac{PBDSI}{BGM2_{-1}} = \underset{(0.0091)}{0.0235} + \underset{(0.0014)}{0.0113\ QS2} + \underset{(0.0013)}{0.0105\ QS3}$$

$$+ \underset{(0.0016)}{0.00163\ QS4} + \underset{(0.0721)}{0.7651} \left(\frac{PBDSI}{BGM2_{-1}}\right)_{-1}$$

$$- \underset{(0.0005)}{0.0021\ ROBLD} - \underset{(0.0377)}{0.0605} \left(\frac{P-P_{-1}}{P-1}\right)$$

$$+ \underset{(0.0212)}{0.0553} \frac{GDPN}{BGM2_{-1}}$$

$$\quad\quad\quad DW = 1.803 \quad\quad R = 0.9911$$

Post-sample lead 1 ARIMA forecasts compared with actual values, BNM forecasts and composite forecasts

(Demand deposits)

		Quarter 1	Quarter 2	Quarter 3	Quarter 4
1971	Actual:	65.40	70.37	73.57	78.14
	Forecast:				
	BNM	63.11	68.14	72.11	77.71
	ARIMA	63.63	68.09	72.90	78.19
	COMPOSITE	63.12	68.15	72.11	77.71
1972	Actual:	75.42	80.20	84.56	90.34
	Forecast:				
	BNM	73.68	77.72	81.46	88.17
	ARIMA	75.32	79.34	83.13	89.46
	COMPOSITE	73.69	77.73	81.46	88.18
1973	Actual:	85.97	86.86	83.64	88.95
	Forecast:				
	BNM	80.75	87.00	86.80	87.56
	ARIMA	87.82	89.91	89.76	87.29
	COMPOSITE	80.76	87.01	86.80	87.57
1974	Actual:	85.47	89.35	91.37	99.63
	Forecast:				
	BNM	80.70	86.31	88.79	94.83
	ARIMA	85.66	87.70	89.28	97.23
	COMPOSITE	80.70	86.32	88.80	94.84

Series 15: Time deposits (PBDTE) in billions of Deutsche Marks

year	Quarter			
	1	2	3	4
1957	47.25	47.78	49.10	50.33
1958	51.45	51.72	52.16	52.23
1959	52.18	52.18	52.70	54.02
1960	54.95	55.55	56.27	56.91
1961	58.79	60.15	60.94	61.66
1962	63.34	64.01	64.37	65.22
1963	66.34	66.77	67.50	69.69
1964	69.93	70.48	70.87	72.02
1965	73.64	73.84	73.36	74.32
1966	78.00	78.58	80.11	81.47
1967	83.84	84.43	84.91	87.14
1968	90.21	92.39	93.66	98.88
1969	103.77	107.17	108.72	111.97
1970	112.73	115.86	120.11	121.82
1971	126.62	130.99	131.05	137.24
1972	142.00	144.10	149.94	157.21
1973	172.46	184.12	195.29	203.94
1974	209.18	210.22	204.15	205.07

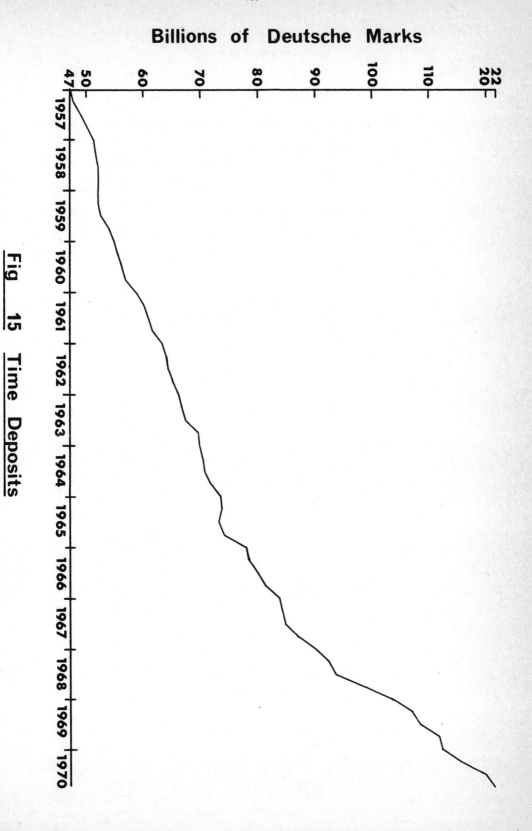

Fig 15 Time Deposits

Autocorrelations and partial autocorrelations
(Time deposits)

	Lags	Autocorrelations				Partial autocorrelations			
z_t	1 - 4	.93	.86	.80	.74	.93	-.05	.00	-.02
	5 - 8	.67	.61	.55	.49	-.05	-.02	-.05	-.02
	9 -12	.43	.39	.34	.29	.01	.01	-.03	-.01
		Mean = 73.57				Var = 420.00			
$\nabla_1 z_t$	1 - 4	.45	.24	.33	.46	.45	.04	.26	.30
	5 - 8	.27	.21	.27	.19	-.06	.06	.05	-.11
	9 -12	.19	.01	.15	.09	.10	-.26	.18	-.10
		Mean = 1.356				Var = 1.514			
$\nabla_1^2 z_t$	1 - 4	-.31	-.28	-.03	.28	-.31	-.42	-.37	-.02
	5 - 8	-.12	-.12	.11	-.06	-.12	-.13	.01	-.20
	9 -12	.18	-.29	.17	.01	.18	-.24	.05	.00
		Mean = .0219				Var = 1.675			
$\nabla_s z_t$	1 - 4	.92	.81	.71	.61	.92	-.34	.17	-.16
	5 - 8	.50	.41	.32	.24	-.08	.03	-.10	.10
	9 -12	.20	.17	.13	.07	.11	-.15	.05	-.21
		Mean = 5.309				Var = 12.59			
$\nabla_1 \nabla_s z_t$	1 - 4	.27	-.02	0.07	-.20	.27	-.10	-.04	-.19
	5 - 8	-.23	-.06	-.07	-.18	-.15	.01	-.11	-.21
	9 -12	.15	.08	.17	.04	.21	-.10	.19	-.17
		Mean = .11				Var = 1.49			

Model identification:

This is a well-behaved series and the autocorrelations suggest a multiplicative seasonal model.

$$(1-B)(1-B^4)z_t = \theta_0 + (1-\theta_1 B)(1-\theta_4 B^4)a_t.$$

Fitting and diagnostic checking:

The fitted model is

$$(1-B)(1-B^4)z_t = .11 + (1+.27B)(1-.60B^4)a_t$$
$$(.14)(.14)$$

$\hat{\sigma}_a = 1.13$; Box-Pierce χ^2 (12-2) = 9.16.

Corresponding econometric model:

$$\frac{PBDTE}{BGM2_{-1}} = 0.0869 - 0.0012 \, QS2 - 0.0025 \, QS3 + 0.0019 \, QS4$$
$$\phantom{\frac{PBDTE}{BGM2_{-1}} =\ }(0.0395)\ (0.0019)(0.0018)(0.0021)$$

$$+ 0.7248 \left(\frac{PBDTE}{BGM2_{-1}}\right)_{-1} + 0.0014 \, RTERM$$
$$(0.1477)\phantom{\left(\frac{PBDTE}{BGM2_{-1}}\right)_{-1}\ }(0.0013)$$

$$-0.0030 \, RBOLD + 0.3070 \, \frac{GB}{BGM2_{-1}} + 4.3564 \, \frac{1}{BGM2_{-1}}$$
$$(0.0022)(0.1437)\phantom{\frac{GB}{BGM2_{-1}}\ + }(0.1037)$$

$$DW = 2.013 \qquad R = 0.9936$$

Post-sample lead 1 ARIMA forecasts compared with actual values, BNM forecasts and composite forecasts
(Time deposits)

		Quarter 1	2	3	4
1971	Actual:	126.62	130.99	131.05	137.24
	Forecast:				
	BNM	124.23	128.16	131.13	134.05
	ARIMA	122.58	130.83	135.28	131.63
	COMPOSITE	124.49	127.59	130.27	134.45
1972	Actual:	142.00	144.10	149.94	157.21
	Forecast:				
	BNM	138.38	141.76	143.99	150.77
	ARIMA	141.10	145.86	146.22	154.42
	COMPOSITE	137.79	140.91	143.49	150.00
1973	Actual:	172.46	184.12	195.29	203.94
	Forecast:				
	BNM	160.66	171.16	178.58	188.93
	ARIMA	161.27	178.48	189.51	201.82
	COMPOSITE	160.46	169.67	176.39	186.35
1974	Actual:	209.18	210.22	204.15	205.07
	Forecast:				
	BNM	195.99	198.12	197.08	196.44
	ARIMA	212.54	214.72	215.78	207.46
	COMPOSITE	192.70	194.82	193.38	194.22

GLOSSARY OF ABBREVIATIONS USED IN THE BONN MONETARY MODELS
(Those not already introduced in the text)

1. ABEXR — Excess reserves
2. BANK — Wealth variable of banks
3. BGM2 — Money (including time and saving deposits)
4. CCAP — Depreciation
5. FXMUS — Swap rate in free market
6. GB — Budget surplus
7. GDPN — GNP in current prices
8. DDPT — Permanent income
9. IFNP — Private fixed investment
10. IPW — World production index
11. NP — Currency outside banks, held by public
12. P — General price level in private sector
13. PBAS — Other foreign liabilities of banks
14. PBDIF — Statistical discrepancy
15. PBIS — Assets (other than foreign) of banks
16. PBREF — Loans to banks held by Bundesbank
17. QS2 — Seasonal dummy (1 for 2nd quarter; 0 otherwise)
18. QS3 — Seasonal dummy (1 for 3rd quarter; 0 otherwise)
19. QS4 — Seasonal dummy (1 for 4th quarter; 0 otherwise)
20. QPROI — Dummy for foreign investment without interest
21. RDISK — Discount rate
22. RLGB — Long-term interest rate in Great Britain
23. ROM — Price of open market paper
24. RSPAR — Rate on saving deposits
25. RSUS — Commercial paper rate in New York
26. RTERM — Rate on time deposits
27. RW — Commercial bill rate
28. SRMAX — Maximum of bank deposits with Bundesbank
29. SRSOL — Required reserves
30. T — Taxes
31. YPPN — Net profit in private sector

INDEX

Autoregressive-integrated moving average (ARIMA) model, 2-8, 10-19

ARIMA forecasts-within sample, 16-19, 21-24

ARIMA forecasts-post-sample, 25, 26, 28, 29

Bates-Granger composite forecast, 6, 20, 29

Bonn econometric model, 7, 9

Bonn Monetary Model (BNM), 7, 10, 11

BNM forecast-within-sample, 16-19, 21-24

BNM forecast-post-sample, 25, 26, 28, 29

Box-Jenkins dynamic model, 41

Box-Pierce χ^2 test, 12-15

Causality-Granger's definition, 30

Conditional efficiency, 7, 20

Endogenous variable, 1, 5

Exogenous variable, 1

Federal Reserve Board-MIT-Pennsylvania model (FMP), 3

Feedback, 31, 34

Final equation, 4

Goodness of fit, 4

Hendry's econometric model, 4

Independence of two series, 37

Instantaneous causality, 31, 34, 40, 41

LINK, 9

London Graduate School of Business Studies Model, 9

Multiplicative Seasonal Model, 12

Noisy-Random Walk model, 12

INDEX continued

Pierce's broad tests, 36

Progressive χ^2 tests, 8, 47, 51

Reduced form, 1

Residual cross correlation, 36

Short-term interest rate, 8, 11, 51

Stochastic model, 2

Structural equation, 1

Two-stage identification, 42

U coefficient, 1, 2

Unidirectional causality, 34, 41

Wharton School Model, 9